THE WORLD
DINOSA

THE WORLD OF THE
DINOSAURS

An exciting guide to prehistoric creatures, with 350
fabulous detailed illustrations of dinosaurs and
prehistoric beasts and the places they lived

DOUGAL DIXON

southwater

This edition is published by Southwater

Southwater is an imprint of Anness Publishing Ltd
Hermes House, 88–89 Blackfriars Road, London SE1 8HA
tel. 020 7401 2077; fax 020 7633 9499
www.southwaterbooks.com
www.annesspublishing.com

If you like the images in this
book and would like to
investigate using them
for publishing, promotions or
advertising, please visit our website
www.practicalpictures.com for more information.

© Anness Publishing Ltd 2007

UK agent: The Manning Partnership Ltd, 6 The Old Dairy
Melcombe Road, Bath BA2 3LR
tel. 01225 478444; fax 01225 478440
sales@manning-partnership.co.uk

UK distributor: Grantham Book Services Ltd
Isaac Newton Way, Alma Park Industrial Estate
Grantham, Lincs NG31 9SD
tel. 01476 541080; fax 01476 541061; orders@gbs.tbs-ltd.co.uk

North American agent/distributor: National Book Network
4501 Forbes Boulevard, Suite 200, Lanham, MD 20706
tel. 301 459 3366; fax 301 429 5746; www.nbnbooks.com

Australian agent/distributor: Pan Macmillan Australia
Level 18, St Martins Tower, 31 Market St, Sydney, NSW 2000
tel. 1300 135 113; fax 1300 135 103
customer.service@macmillan.com.au

New Zealand agent/distributor: David Bateman Ltd
30 Tarndale Grove, Off Bush Road, Albany, Auckland
tel. (09) 415 7664; fax (09) 415 8892

Publisher: Joanna Lorenz
Editorial Director: Helen Sudell
Project Editor: Simona Hill
Designer: Nigel Partridge
Illustrators: Peter Barrett, Alain Beneteau, Andrey Atuchin,
Anthony Duke, Stuart Jackson-Carter, Julius Csotonyi
Editorial Reader: Rosanna Fairhead and Lindsay Zamponi
Production Controller: Lee Sargent

ETHICAL TRADING POLICY

At Anness Publishing we believe that business should be
conducted in an ethical and ecologically sustainable way, with
respect for the environment and a proper regard to the replacement
of the natural resources we employ.

As a publisher, we use a lot of wood pulp to make high-quality
paper for printing, and that wood commonly comes from spruce
trees. We are therefore currently growing more than 500,000 trees
in two Scottish forest plantations near Aberdeen – Berrymoss (130
hectares/320 acres) and West Touxhill (125 hectares/305 acres).
The forests we manage contain twice the number of trees
employed each year in paper-making for our books.

Because of this ongoing ecological investment programme, you, as
our customer, can have the pleasure and reassurance of knowing
that a tree is being cultivated on your behalf to naturally replace the
materials used to make the book you are holding.

Our forestry programme is run in accordance with the UK
Woodland Assurance Scheme (UKWAS) and will be certified by the
internationally recognized Forest Stewardship Council (FSC). The
FSC is a non-government organization dedicated to promoting
responsible management of the world's forests. Certification
ensures forests are managed in an environmentally sustainable and
socially responsible basis. For further information about this
scheme, go to www.annesspublishing.com/trees

Previously published as part of a larger volume, *The
Illustrated Encyclopedia of Dinosaurs*

10 9 8 7 6 5 4 3 2 1

CONTENTS

INTRODUCTION

Above: A mother Shanxia *guards her offspring against a desert sandstorm.*

The science of paleontology (the study of dinosaurs) is developing at an exciting speed. New discoveries are being made so quickly, that before this book is on the bookshelves there will have been an overwhelming number of new finds and developments in the understanding of the subject. Each week there is something new to report, whether it be a skeleton that constitutes an entirely new branch of the dinosaur evolutionary tree, or some indication of the dinosaurs' life gleaned through new finds of footprints or feeding traces. Microscopic analysis of fossilized dinosaur dung has recently provided new information about dinosaur diet and the plants of the contemporary landscape.

In total about 500 dinosaur species have been identified. The majority of these are based on only a scrap of bone or a tooth or some such small piece of evidence. This

Right: Phuwiangosaurus, *from the early Cretaceous is known from Thailand.*

figure represents those species that have been found, excavated, studied and described scientifically. Many more are likely to be found by the next generation of palaeontologists.

Our knowledge of dinosaurs is weighted towards those that we know existed close to rivers, or in deserts, or on the banks of lakes or lagoons – places where dead bodies are likely to have been buried quickly and fossilized. We do not have direct evidence yet of the dinosaurs that lived on mountains or highland forests, or other places that were far from quick burial sites.

Estimates have been made about the number of dinosaurs that actually existed. Mathematical formulae have been applied using such factors as the speed at which new discoveries are being made today compared with the speed at which they were made by earlier palaeontologists, the larger areas that are now being explored worldwide compared with the early history of the science, the different habitats and land areas that existed during dinosaur times, and so on. One result estimated that 1,500 dinosaur species existed.

The book provides an overview of the Age of Dinosaurs, introducing the key areas of research that have helped paleontologists to paint a picture of

what the world was like in dinosaur times. From fossil evidence, we can say with certainty much about how the dinosaurs lived, what food they ate, whether they lived in groups, had family networks, and what the landscape looked like.

This is followed by a selection of the dinosaurs that are currently known to have existed. The Age of Dinosaurs, known as the Mesozoic Era (a reference to the rock formations in which the dinosaurs have been found) is divided into three periods – Triassic (representing the earliest period of dinosaur history), Jurassic and Cretaceous (the latest period of dinosaur history). These periods of time are subdivided further.

Fascinating information about each dinosaur entry is provided and is accompanied by a concise description of the features that make the animal distinctive. A fact box lists some of the technical data, such as the period of history when the animal lived, its dimensions and its discoverer. Each is illustrated with a beautiful watercolour that shows what the animal looked like. The appearance is based on the evidence available, sometimes gained from

Below: Masiakasaurus *is an unusual abelisaurid from Madagascar.*

only a single bone, utilizing studies of related animals to make the best attempt possible of a restoration of the living beast.

In science an animal is known by its scientific name, or its "binomial". For example, humans are scientifically known as *Homo sapiens*. *Homo* is the genus name and *sapiens* is the species name. The names, usually derived from Latin or classical Greek, are always italicized with only the genus name capitalized. For dinosaurs it is customary to use only the genus name in popular literature. *Tyrannosaurus rex*, however, is so evocative that often both are used. Once the genus name has been introduced, it can then be referred to by its genus initial along with its species name. Hence *T. rex*. In many instances a particular dinosaur genus has several species. This should help to explain the usage of names in this encyclopedia. Here you will find animals that have never been portrayed before, with facts and illustrations based on the analysis of the most up-to-date scientific papers.

Left: A herd of Monoclonius *flee a forest fire. Little dramas like these can be deduced from the fossil record.*

1 *Oviraptor*.
2 Pterosaur.
3 *Velociraptor*.
4 Baby *Oviraptor*.
5 *Ornithoides*.

THE AGE OF DINOSAURS

The dinosaurs lived between 220 and 65 million years ago. Science can give us a good idea of what the Age of Dinosaurs was like. For the past two centuries, dinosaur bones and traces have been dug up and studied, and every discovery adds some new information to what we already know.

The physical bones, mineralized and preserved as fossils, provide the main clues to what the dinosaurs looked like. However, the scientific interpretation of these fossils has changed over the decades – what we would construct now from the bones would not be recognizable to the Victorian scientists who first unearthed them.

The soft anatomy of skin, muscles and tissues is rarely fossilized, but when it is, it provides a valuable insight to the anatomical make up of the dinosaur. When we compare this with the anatomy of living animals, it is possible to understand how that dinosaur functioned.

Other lines of evidence show us how dinosaurs lived. Fossil dung can be analyzed to establish what they ate. We can also examine tooth marks on the bones of the animals killed and eaten by the dinosaurs.

Fossil footprints are the remains of dinosaur movements. A whole branch of the science of palaeontology is dedicated to the study of these trackways and what they can tell us about how dinosaurs moved. There is also evidence of their family groups and the social structure within which dinosaurs lived. Over the years eggs and nests have been found in various places around the world, and these help paleontologists build up a picture of family life and colonies.

Of course, dinosaurs lived in more than one place and collectively lived over millions of years. Different habitats were home to different dinosaur types, and these environments produced different modes of fossilization of their remains. Nonetheless all these lines of evidence give us an image of what conditions were like for the dinosaurs, and for the other animals that lived alongside them. Consequently, we can produce a landscape of dinosaur life within known habitats, and be confident in its accuracy.

Welcome to the Age of Dinosaurs.

Left: The Gobi Desert, 100 million years ago, late Cretaceous period. Dinosaurs hunt for food, fight over prey and look after their young.

THE GEOLOGICAL TIMESCALE

Geological time is an unbelievably massive concept to grasp. Millions of years, tens of millions of years, hundreds of millions of years. These unfathomable stretches of time are often referred to as "deep time". This is the scale that palaeontologists and anyone interested in dinosaurs must use.

When did dinosaurs appear? About 220,000,000 years ago. And when did they die out? About 65,000,000 years ago. It is easier when we say 220 million and 65 million, but we could use a better system.

To make the concept easier, geologists and palaeontologists have always split geological time into named periods. It is the same when we talk about human history. We can say 150 years ago, or 200 years ago, or 600 years ago, but it gives a clearer idea of the time if we say Victorian London, or Napoleonic Europe or Pre-Columbian North America – then we can put events into their chronological context.

Geological time periods are named after the rock sequences that were formed at that time, and the names were given by the scientists (mostly Victorian, about 150 years ago) who first studied them in the regions in which they typically outcrop.

The periods that concern anyone interested in dinosaurs are the Triassic (so named because the rocks of that time were identified as three separate sequences in Germany), the Jurassic (named after the Jura Mountains, on the border of France and Switzerland, where they were first studied), and the Cretaceous (named after the Latin for chalk, the most prominent rock type formed at that time in southern England). Collectively the three periods are known as the Mesozoic era. Each period encompasses tens of millions of years, so is further subdivided into stages for ease of reference. The stages are given at the bottom of the facing page, along with the actual number of years that they entailed, so that they can be referred to when necessary. The stages are then divided into zones, but these time divisions are too small to be of any interest to us here.

Above: A fossil forms when an animal dies and its body falls into sediment that is accumulating at the time. The body is buried and the organic matter of the hard parts is transformed into mineral at the same time as the sediment is transformed into sedimentary rock. The pterosaur shown must have died while it was flying over a shallow lagoon in late Jurassic times. It sank to the bottom of the lagoon, where it was buried by contemporary sediment.

There are two ways in which geological events are dated. The first is "relative dating" – placing events on the geological time scale in relation to each other. This is the principle involved in most studies of the past. Fossil A is found in rocks that lie

Below: The age of the Earth is so immense that it can only be shown diagrammatically in some kind of distorted image. The Earth's origin can be placed about 4,600 million years ago, but the part that really interests palaeontologists begins about 590 million years ago. Since that time the geography of the Earth has changed, with the continents constantly moving to new positions.

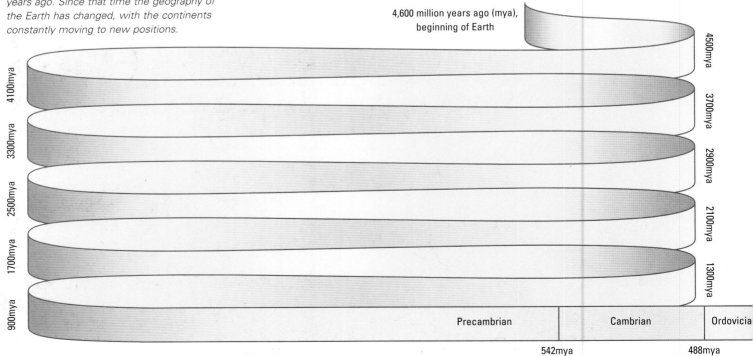

4,600 million years ago (mya), beginning of Earth

4100mya 3300mya 2500mya 1700mya 900mya

4500mya 3700mya 2900mya 2100mya 1300mya

Precambrian | Cambrian | Ordovicia

542mya 488mya

above those in which fossil B is found. That means that fossil B is older than fossil A; in an undisturbed sequence of sedimentary rocks the oldest is always on the bottom. If a fossil is found in a rock on another continent from which that fossil is usually found, then the two rocks will be of the same age, even if there are no other clues to the age of the rocks. The fossil dates the rock.

The second type of geological dating is absolute dating. This is much more tricky, and involves studying the decay of radioactive minerals in a particular rock. A radioactive mineral breaks down at a particular known rate. If we can measure the amount of that mineral remaining, and compare it with the amount of what is called the "decay residue", we can tell how long

Above: Geological periods are defined by the fossils found in the sedimentary rocks formed at that particular time. Sedimentary rocks are those that are built up from layers of mud and sand, and have been compressed and solidified over time. Those shown here represent an angular unconformity between two rock formations: Triassic rocks are the horizontal ones lying above Devonian rocks, which are inclined at 40 degrees. These were laid down horizontally, but have been tilted by movements under the surface.

Below: The three periods of the Mesozoic era, the Triassic, the Jurassic and the Cretaceous, are the periods in which the dinosaurs lived. They evolved in the latter part of the Triassic and died out at the end of the Cretaceous. These periods are further divided into stages.

When geologists refer to different parts of a period, they talk about "upper" Cretaceous or "lower" Jurassic. This is a reference to the rock sequence in which the rocks formed. When we talk about the events that took place at these times, we use the terms "late" Cretaceous or "early" Jurassic instead.

it has been decaying and how long ago it formed. Several radioactive elements are used in this method.

One disconcerting aspect about geological time, however, is that the absolute dates keep changing. This is because the science used to determine them becomes increasingly sophisticated and precise with developments in technology and understanding. A century ago we were talking in terms of tens of millions of years, whereas nowadays the same periods are talked of in hundreds of millions of years. This is why dates may differ in various dinosaur books.

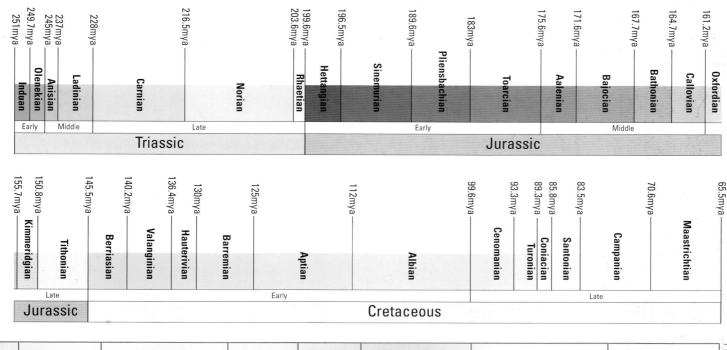

Triassic / Jurassic timescale

Stage	Date	Epoch	Period
Induan	251mya	Early	Triassic
Olenekian	249.7mya	Early	Triassic
Anisian	245mya	Middle	Triassic
Ladinian	237mya	Middle	Triassic
Carnian	228mya	Late	Triassic
Norian	216.5mya	Late	Triassic
Rhaetian	203.6mya	Late	Triassic
Hettangian	199.6mya	Early	Jurassic
Sinemurian	196.5mya	Early	Jurassic
Pliensbachian	189.6mya	Early	Jurassic
Toarcian	183mya	Early	Jurassic
Aalenian	175.6mya	Middle	Jurassic
Bajocian	171.6mya	Middle	Jurassic
Bathonian	167.7mya	Middle	Jurassic
Callovian	164.7mya	Middle	Jurassic
Oxfordian	161.2mya	Middle	Jurassic

Jurassic / Cretaceous timescale

Stage	Date	Epoch	Period
Kimmeridgian	155.7mya	Late	Jurassic
Tithonian	150.8mya	Late	Jurassic
Berriasian	145.5mya	Early	Cretaceous
Valanginian	140.2mya	Early	Cretaceous
Hauterivian	136.4mya	Early	Cretaceous
Barremian	130mya	Early	Cretaceous
Aptian	125mya	Early	Cretaceous
Albian	112mya	Early	Cretaceous
Cenomanian	99.6mya	Late	Cretaceous
Turonian	93.3mya	Late	Cretaceous
Coniacian	89.3mya	Late	Cretaceous
Santonian	85.8mya	Late	Cretaceous
Campanian	83.5mya	Late	Cretaceous
Maastrichtian	70.6mya	Late	Cretaceous
	65.5mya		

Overall timescale

Silurian	Devonian	Carboniferous	Permian	Triassic	Jurassic	Cretaceous	Tertiary	Present
416mya	359.2mya	299mya	251mya	199.6mya	145.5mya	65.5mya		

EARLY EVOLUTION

Where did life come from? We are not quite sure, but it seems that living things of one kind or another have been around since the Earth was cool enough to have liquid water on its surface. The process of evolution has meant that there has been an uninterrupted stream of living creatures ever since then.

What is life? There are several definitions, but each agrees that a living thing absorbs materials and energy, grows and reproduces. The tiniest bacteria and single cells conform to this definition, and these are the living things that existed way back when the Earth had just begun to cool.

By far the greatest part of Earth's history is encompassed by Precambrian time, but there is little direct evidence about what living things were like then. Bacteria and single-celled organisms do not leave much in the way of fossils. However, we have indirect evidence that things lived then, and gradually evolved into soft-bodied, multi-cellular creatures during that period. This vast span of time is called the Cryptozoic, meaning "the time of hidden life". The end of the Precambrian period (542 million years ago) and the beginning of the fossil record proper is usually marked by an event called the "Cambrian explosion".

At this time, the beginning of the Cambrian period, evolution perfected the hard shell. Organisms had the ability to absorb the mineral calcite from the seawater and lay it down as a living shell, or from organic compounds they built up a kind of natural plastic called chitin – the material from which our fingernails are made. This had two results. First it meant that there was suddenly a kind of evolutionary arms race. Animals had always been hunting and eating one another. Now some animals could defend themselves, and consequently the hunters evolved new structures and techniques to get the upper hand.

Evolution in the ocean

Suddenly the oceans (for all life was in the oceans at this time) were full of all kinds of creatures that had not existed before. And what strange beasts they were! There were animals with many legs or none, with shelled heads, with shelled tails, with spikes, and with burrowing tools – it was as if nature was trying out anything just to see what worked. By the end of the Cambrian period this vast array of strange beings had whittled itself down to a dozen or so well-tried evolutionary lines that have continued until the present day. The second result of evolution producing hard shells was based on the fact that hard-shelled animals leave good fossils. The history of life from that point forward is well documented, which is why the time span from the Cambrian to the present day is called the Phanerozoic (meaning "obvious life").

One of the surviving strands of life consisted of worm-like animals with a nervous system running down their length, supported by a jointed framework. The brain was at the front, protected by a box. The mouth and sensory organs were also at the front. From simple animals like this evolved the first vertebrates, the first animals with backbones.

The first vertebrates

Fish were the first vertebrates that we would recognize, and they came to prominence in Ordovician and Silurian times (488–443 million years ago).

The first fish are known as the "jawless fish". Rather like the modern

Below: Evidence of life in the Precambrian period (more than 590 million years ago) is vague. However, what we do know is that all the major evolutionary lines of living things had evolved by the dawn of the Cambrian period (590 million years ago) and were leaving their imprint on the Earth, as well-preserved fossils.
The vast majority of animals at this time, both living and fossil, are invertebrates.

Soft-bodied

Chordates
Brachiopods
Echinoderms
Hemichordates
Sponges
Jellyfish
Corals
Flatworms
Molluscs
Annelids
Arthropods

PRECAMBRIAN, 542 MILLION YEARS AGO CAMBRIAN, 542–488 MILLION YEARS AGO

lamprey, they had a sucker instead of jaws, and they probably lived by sucking up nutritious debris from the seafloor as they swam along. A fin along the underside of the tail ensured that they swam head down. Proper jaws and a more organized skeleton then developed. The first skeletons were not made of bone but of cartilage. The cartilaginous fish are represented today by the sharks and rays. They appeared in Silurian times.

The next stage was the evolution of bone around the cartilage framework. Bone formed the skeleton and also the armour plates for protection. Then came the kinds of scales we would recognize from the fish we see today. These bony, armoured fish, and the scaly fish, appeared in the Devonian period. By this time there were so many different fish that the Devonian period (416–359 million years ago) is often termed the "Age of Fishes".

A changing environment

Meanwhile, changes were taking place out of the water. In early Precambrian times the atmosphere was a bitter mix of noxious gases, which is why all early life evolved in the sea. Gradually the by-products of early living systems were seeping into the atmosphere and changing it. Oxygen, a product of the photosynthesis process, which keeps plants alive,

started to build up in the atmosphere and make land habitable. The first green patches of land appeared between tides probably during Silurian times. When plants pioneered life on land, animals followed behind. One kind of fish developed lungs to enable it to breathe the oxygen of the atmosphere. It also developed paired muscular fins that would allow it to crawl on a solid surface as well as swim in the water. The vertebrates were poised to take a step on to the land. As soon as the continents became habitable, life spread there from the oceans, and a vast array of animals have been present ever since.

Life on land

Creatures had been venturing out on to land for hundreds of millions of years. Tracks of arthropods (the first land-living animals) are known from beach sediments formed in Ordovician times. There are mysterious marks from dry land deposits that look like motor-cycle tracks back in the Cambrian period. They seem to have been tentative explorations, but it does not appear that animal life out of the water was permanent until plants had gained a foothold. Insects and spiders infested the primitive early plants that clothed the sides of streams in the Silurian period. The first fish ventured out in the subsequent Devonian time.

It is not clear why fish first appeared on land. Some scientists say that the newly evolved arthropod fauna that had established itself among the plants was too tempting a food source to be ignored. Others suggest that land-living was an emergency measure – if a fish became trapped in a drying puddle of water it would need to be able to survive and travel over land to find more water in which it could live. There is also a theory that the waters became too dangerous due to predatory animals; there were clawed arthropods as big as alligators at the time, and some fish found it safer to take up a land-living existence.

Eusthenopteron was typical of the kind of fish that was able to spend time on land. The major adaptation was the lung. Fish normally breathe through gills – feathery structures that can filter dissolved oxygen from the water. Now lungs enabled oxygen to be extracted directly from the air. Then there was the manner of

Below: By Ordovician (488–443 million years ago) and Silurian (443–416 million years ago) times the backboned animals had evolved, in the form of the most primitive fish. The backbone supported the whole body, the limbs were arranged in pairs at the side, and the brain was encased in a box of bone. The next stage came when these swimming animals evolved to be able to breathe air.

Jawless fish

Cartilagenous fish

locomotion. A typical fish's fin consists of a ray of supports with a web between, spreading from a muscular stump. In *Eusthenopteron* and its relatives the fins consisted of muscular lobes, supported by a network of bones, with the fin material forming mere fringes along the edge. Two pairs were arranged on the underside of the body, and they could be used both for swimming and for heaving the animal across open land.

The first amphibians

By the end of the Devonian period, the next stage in the evolution of land vertebrates had been accomplished, and the first amphibian-like animals appeared. These animals were much more complex in their variety and relationships than the single term "amphibian" implies. *Ichthyostega* was one of the earliest of these animals. The difference between *Ichthyostega* and the lobe-finned fish was in the limbs. Now the fins were clearly jointed, with leg and toe bones. It seems likely that they evolved for pulling the animal along through weeds in shallow water, but they were ideal for clambering on land as well. The *Ichthyostega* foot was odd by

Below: .Many of the evolutionary lines that existed at the start of the Precambrian continued to evolve. Some evolutionary lines, such as the armoured fish, ceased to exist. Other lines split with new creatures evolving and beginning new evolutionary lines.

modern standards because there were eight toes. The standard arrangement of a maximum of five toes for a land-living vertebrate had yet to be established. For all its land-living abilities, *Ichthyostega* and its relatives still had the head and tail of a fish, and had to return to the water to breed.

The next great advance in evolution was the ability of animals to breed on land. This was achieved by the first of the amniotes, named after the amnion – the membrane that contained the developing young within the egg. A hard-shelled egg evolved, that nourished the young in what was essentially a self-contained watery pond, that could be laid away from the water. At last the link with the ancestral seas was severed. Early examples include *Westlothiana* from Scotland and *Hylonomus* from Nova Scotia, both dating from the early Carboniferous period.

The first reptiles

The true reptiles then established themselves along a number of evolutionary branches. In the simplest form of classification they can be classified by the number and arrangement of holes in the skull behind the eye socket. The anapsids had no such holes because the skull was a solid roof of bone behind the

eye. The anapsids were prominent in the Permian period in a group called the pareiasaurs. Modern relatives of pareiasaurs include tortoises and turtles.

The synapsids, however, had a single hole in the skull at each side. They became the mammal-like reptiles, the major group of the Permian period. When they died away in Triassic times they lived on as the humble mammals, and did not really come to prominence again until the Tertiary period.

The diapsids were different because they had two holes behind the eye. Modern diapsids include snakes, crocodiles and lizards. However, a group of Mesozoic (the combined Triassic, Jurassic and Cretaceous periods) diapsids was much more important. They evolved into the dinosaurs.

Dinosaur evolution

The dinosaurs evolved from the diapsid line that we call the archosaurs, meaning the ruling reptiles. Other archosaurs were the pterosaurs, and the crocodiles and alligators that we have today. A typical Triassic archosaur was a swift, two-footed, running meat-eater, usually no bigger than a wolf and usually much smaller. In fact an advanced archosaur would have looked very much like a typical,

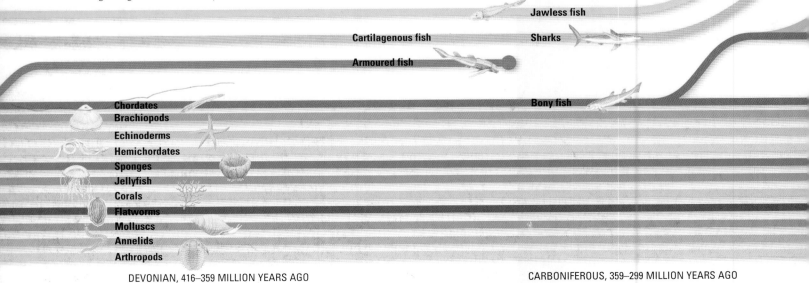

Jawless fish

Cartilagenous fish

Sharks

Armoured fish

Bony fish

Chordates
Brachiopods
Echinoderms
Hemichordates
Sponges
Jellyfish
Corals
Flatworms
Molluscs
Annelids
Arthropods

DEVONIAN, 416–359 MILLION YEARS AGO   CARBONIFEROUS, 359–299 MILLION YEARS AGO

small, meat-eating dinosaur. What made the dinosaur different from its archosaurian ancestor lay mostly in the structure of the leg and hips.

Most reptiles have legs that stick out at the side, with the weight of the animal slung between them. This gives the animal a sprawling gait. To enable it to run quickly it must throw its body into S-shaped curves to give the sideways-pointing limbs the reach that is needed. In contrast, a dinosaur's leg was straight and vertical. It was plugged into the side of the hip where it was held in place by a shelf of bone.

This meant that a dinosaur's weight was at the top of the leg, and transmitted straight downwards. Vertical limbs can support a greater weight than sprawling limbs. This is the arrangement that we see in a typical mammal, and this upright stance is seen in all dinosaurs, whether two- or four-legged.

Saurischians and ornithischians
So, the first dinosaur was probably like an archosaur, and good at running. From there dinosaur evolution

diverged into two main lines – the saurischia and the ornithischia. The difference between the two lines lies in the structure of the hips.

The saurischia had hip bones arranged like those of a lizard, a structure that radiated from the leg bone socket, with a pubis bone that pointed down and forward. This line is further divided into two groups; the first group developed along the evolutionary line pioneered by the earlier archosaurs, the two-footed hunters. They were termed theropods

Below: As the fish developed into more complex forms, some became land dwellers, with jointed limbs and lungs able to breathe the air. These became the first amphibians. From them, evolved animals able to live on land all the time, without resorting to water at any stage in their growth. The reptiles, with their hard-shelled eggs, represented this stage, and they diversified into all kinds of land-living types.

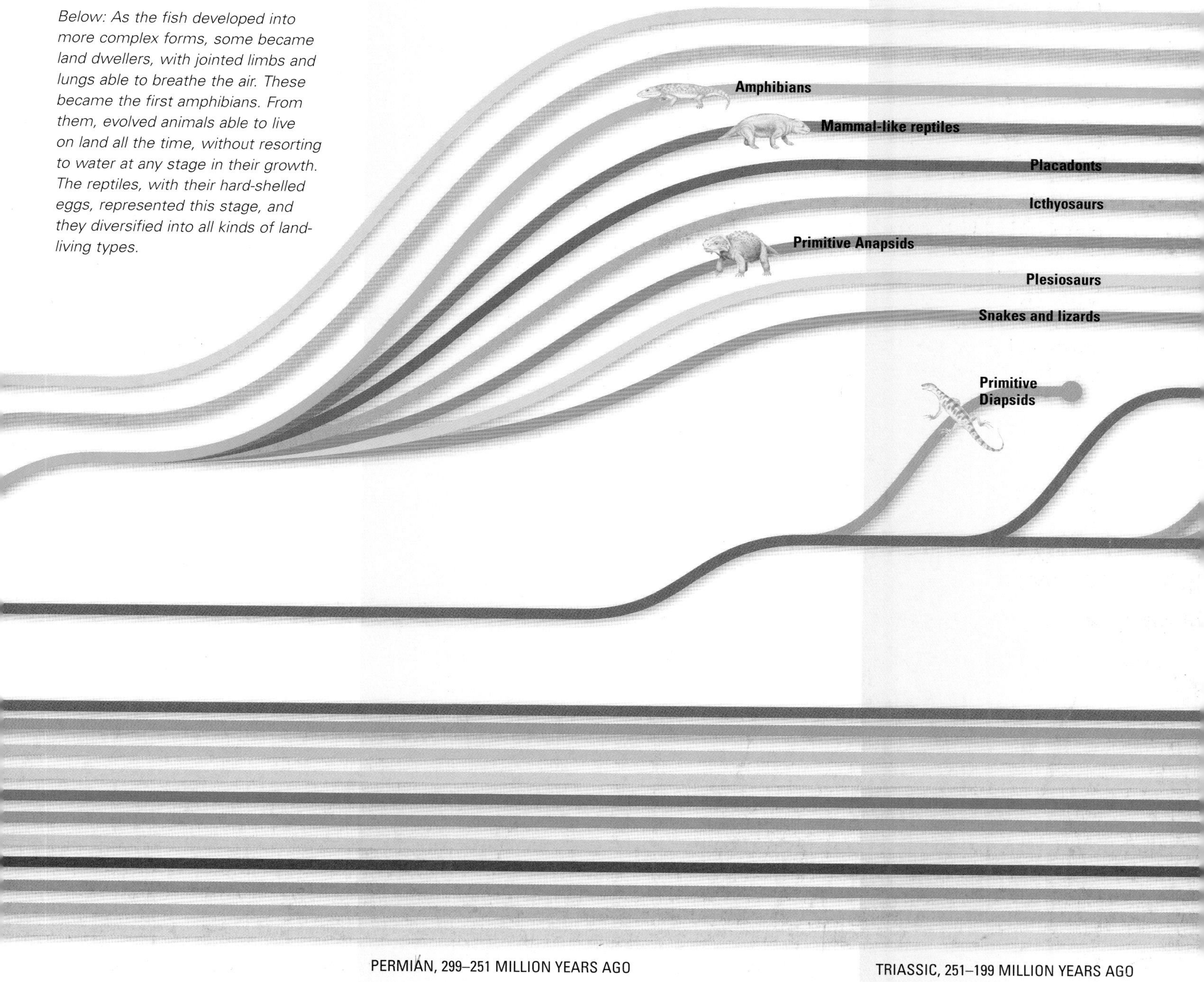

Amphibians

Mammal-like reptiles

Placadonts

Icthyosaurs

Primitive Anapsids

Plesiosaurs

Snakes and lizards

Primitive Diapsids

PERMIAN, 299–251 MILLION YEARS AGO

TRIASSIC, 251–199 MILLION YEARS AGO

or "beast-footed", by the Victorian scientists who detected a similarity between their foot bones and the bones of mammals. All the meat-eating dinosaurs were theropods, from small chicken-size scampering insect-eaters, to massive 15m- (50ft-) long beasts.

The other saurischian group are the sauropods, meaning "lizard-footed", and so called because of the similarity in the structure of the foot to that of a modern lizard. They were the huge, long-necked plant-eaters of the dinosaur world, and their body shape evolved in response to a changing vegetarian diet. The shape of the saurischian hip, with its forward-pointing pubis bone, meant that the big digestive system of a plant-eater had to be carried in front of the hind legs. The result is an animal that would be unable to walk solely on its hind legs, and in response the smaller front legs became stronger to take the weight. This development reduced the mobility of the animal, and so a long neck developed to enable it to reach enough food. As a group of dinosaurs sauropods encompass the biggest land animals that ever existed.

Below: The dinosaurs, once they evolved, soon developed into a number of distinctive groups. Some were meat-eaters, others were plant-eaters. Some moved on four legs and others on two. They were the most significant land animals of the time – between the late Triassic and the end of the Cretaceous. However, at the end of the Cretaceous they, and many other animal groups, became extinct.

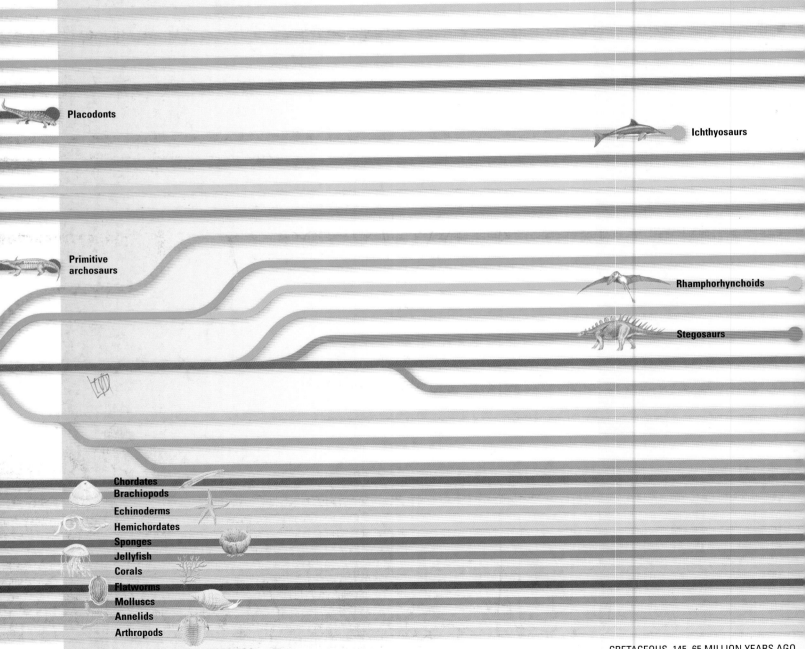

Placodonts

Ichthyosaurs

Primitive archosaurs

Rhamphorhynchoids

Stegosaurs

Chordates
Brachiopods
Echinoderms
Hemichordates
Sponges
Jellyfish
Corals
Flatworms
Molluscs
Annelids
Arthropods

JURASSIC, 199–145 MILLION YEARS AGO

CRETACEOUS, 145–65 MILLION YEARS AGO

The second line of dinosaurs was the ornithischians. They were plant-eaters but had a different arrangement of hip bones. The pubis bone was swept back and lay along the backward-facing ischium bone. This meant the typical ornithischian could carry the weight of its body beneath the hips, and so it could still walk on its hind legs balanced by the heavy tail. A typical two-footed ornithischian was the ornithopod, the bird-footed dinosaur with three splayed toes.

The sauropods and ornithopods also had different eating methods. The sauropods could not chew their food they had to eat so much that they would not have had time to. Their teeth showed that they raked leaves and twigs from the branches and swallowed what they took without processing it. In contrast, ornithopods had teeth that could chew food thoroughly before swallowing it.

Other developments from the basic ornithopod involved the development of armour. The stegosaurs had plates, the ankylosaurs had armour, and the ceratopsians had horns.

Mammals

After 160 million years, the dinosaurs became extinct, but not before the theropods gave rise to the birds. The way was open for the mammals. Since the end of the Cretaceous, the mammals have expanded and occupied all ecological niches once occupied by the dinosaurs.

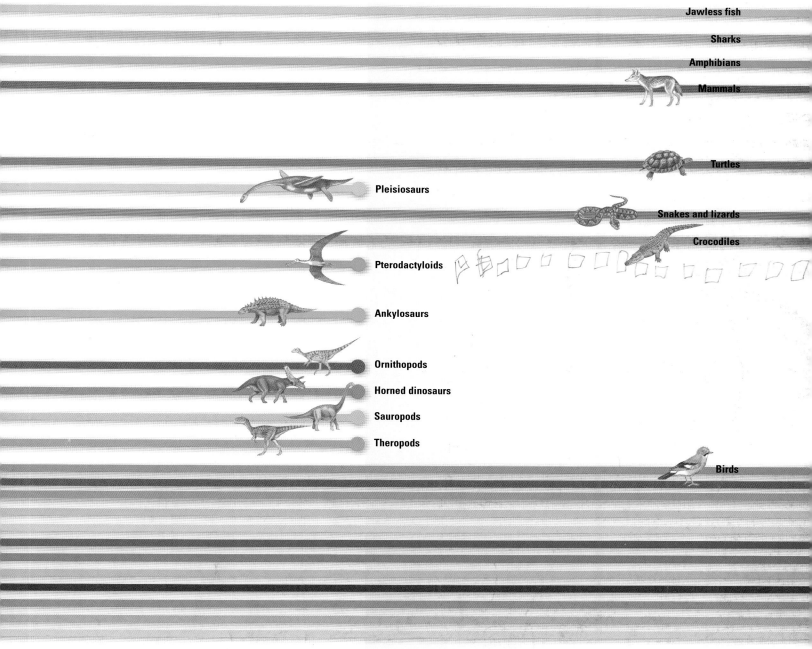

Jawless fish

Sharks

Amphibians

Mammals

Turtles

Pleisiosaurs

Snakes and lizards

Crocodiles

Pterodactyloids

Ankylosaurs

Ornithopods

Horned dinosaurs

Sauropods

Theropods

Birds

TERTIARY, 65 MILLION YEARS AGO–PRESENT DAY

DINOSAUR CLASSIFICATION

The various dinosaurs evolved from common ancestors – in technical terms they were "monophyletic".
Early in their evolution they split into two major evolutionary lines, and these in turn split into a number
of different families, each with its own character and specialization.

The dinosaurs fall into two major groups – the saurischians and the ornithischians. The saurischians are divided into the plant-eating sauropodomorphs and the meat-eating theropods, while the latter are divided into a number of different plant-eating types. Note that the formal classifications (e.g. Theropoda) are used interchangeably with the less formal (e.g. theropods) throughout the book. This is customary in palaeontology.

Dinosauria
The ruling reptiles are characterized by:
• The number of bones in the skull.
• The presence of a flange on the upper arm bone that held powerful muscles.
• Three or fewer finger bones in the fourth finger.
• Three or more vertebrae fixed to the hip bones.
• A hole rather than a socket in the hip for the leg bone.
• A ball-like head on the thigh bone.
• A strong joint between the foot bones and the bones of the hind leg.

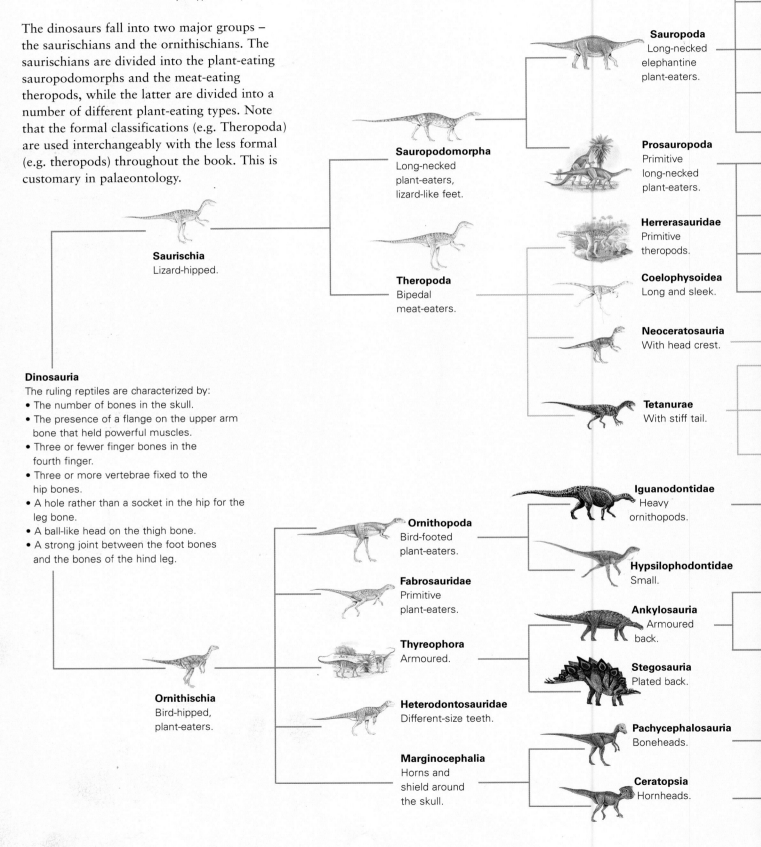

Saurischia
Lizard-hipped.

Sauropodomorpha
Long-necked plant-eaters, lizard-like feet.

Theropoda
Bipedal meat-eaters.

Sauropoda
Long-necked elephantine plant-eaters.

Prosauropoda
Primitive long-necked plant-eaters.

Herrerasauridae
Primitive theropods.

Coelophysoidea
Long and sleek.

Neoceratosauria
With head crest.

Tetanurae
With stiff tail.

Ornithischia
Bird-hipped, plant-eaters.

Ornithopoda
Bird-footed plant-eaters.

Fabrosauridae
Primitive plant-eaters.

Thyreophora
Armoured.

Heterodontosauridae
Different-size teeth.

Marginocephalia
Horns and shield around the skull.

Iguanodontidae
Heavy ornithopods.

Hypsilophodontidae
Small.

Ankylosauria
Armoured back.

Stegosauria
Plated back.

Pachycephalosauria
Boneheads.

Ceratopsia
Hornheads.

Vulcanodontidae
Primitive.

Macronaria
Big nostrils.

Titanosauria
Late-evolving. Mostly
from the Southern
Hemisphere.

Diplodocidae
Long neck and whip tail.

Euhelopodidae
Very long neck.

Dicraeosauridae
Tall spines on the
backbone.

Cetiosauridae
Solid vertebrae.

Massospondylidae
Long bones in the neck.

Plateosauridae
Medium-size.

Melanorosauridae
Large.

Abelisauria
Late, evolving.
Mostly from the
Southern
Hemisphere.

Anchisauridae
Small.

Compsognathidae
Small.

Therizinosauria
Big claws on the hands.

Troodontidae
Swift, killing claw on the toe.

Ornithomimosauria
Ostrich-like.

Oviraptorosauria
Toothless beak.

Alvarezsauria
Stunted forelimbs.

Coelurosauria
Lightweight bones.

Deinonychosauria
Big killing claw on the
second toe.

Carnosauria
Widespread meat-eaters.

Spinosauria
Sail on back, crocodile
jaws.

Allosauridae
Big meat-eaters.

Tyrannosauroidea
Large, late-evolving.

Hadrosauridea
Duck bill.

Lambeosaurinae
Hollow crest.

Edmontosaurini
No crest.

Hadrosaurinae
Solid crest
or none at all.

Maiasaurini
Broad, solid crest
above the eyes.

Nodosauridae
Spikes along their
sides, and a
narrow snout.

Polacanthidae
Spikes on the
shoulders and
shields on the hips.

Saurolophini
Pointed crest at the
top of the skull.

Ankylosauridae
Broad snout.

Ankylosaurinae
Clubs on the end
of the tail.

Hadrosaurini
Bulbous nose.

Pachycephalosaurini
Boneheads with
knobs and horns.

Centrosaurinae
Single horn on
the nose.

Neoceratopsia
Early, two-footed
hornheads.

Ceratopsidae
Big horned head.

Ceratopsinae
Horns over
the eyes.

Chasmosaurini
Very large neck
frill.

THEROPODS

All the meat-eating dinosaurs belonged to the theropod group. They all conformed to a similar body plan. They had a small body and walked on two legs. The head was held out at the front and was balanced by a heavy tail. The arms were small and used for grasping or killing. The hand usually had three fingers.

The theropods appeared at the beginning of the Age of Dinosaurs, in the latter part of the Triassic period. In appearance the early theropods would have resembled their thecodont ancestors. The thecodonts are the reptile group that had teeth in sockets, rather than in grooves as lizards had. The main differences would have been in the stance of the legs and the structure of the skull. The thecodonts had been active hunters, and the early theropods carried on this tradition.

A theropod is an ideal shape for a hunter. The head, jaws and teeth are carried well forward, and are the first part of the animal to make contact with its prey. The arms and the claws are also well forward. The body is quite small, as befits a meat-eating animal. The legs are powerful, with strong muscles working against the bones of the lizard-like hips. The tail is big and heavy, used for balancing and keeping the upper body well forward.

We know that at least some of the theropods were warm-blooded. The term warm-blooded does not necessarily refer to the temperature of the blood, but instead implies that a mechanism exists that keeps the animal's body at the same temperature regardless of the temperature of its surroundings. Nowadays warm-bloodedness is found in mammals and birds, the direct descendants of the theropods.

Warm- or cold-blooded?

Whether or not a dinosaur was warm-blooded is of great significance to understanding its lifestyle. A warm-blooded animal needs ten times as

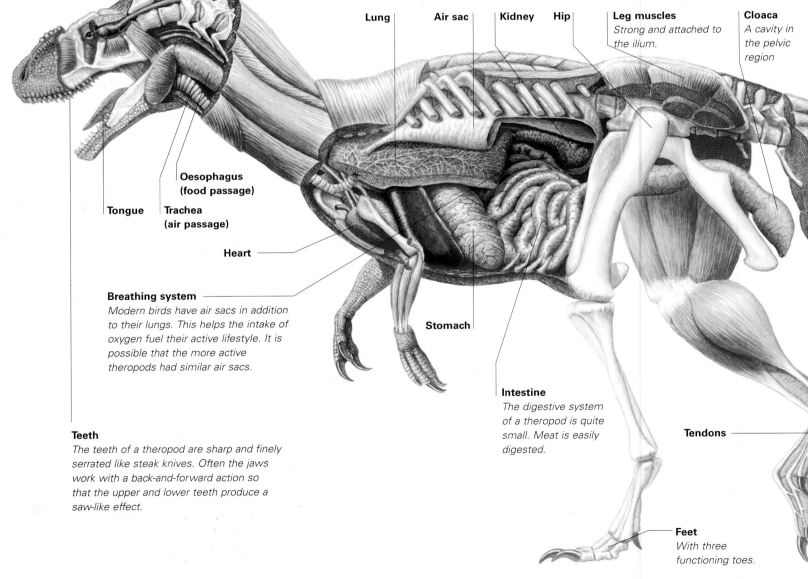

Lung

Air sac

Kidney

Hip

Leg muscles
Strong and attached to the ilium.

Cloaca
A cavity in the pelvic region

Oesophagus (food passage)

Tongue

Trachea (air passage)

Heart

Breathing system
Modern birds have air sacs in addition to their lungs. This helps the intake of oxygen fuel their active lifestyle. It is possible that the more active theropods had similar air sacs.

Stomach

Intestine
The digestive system of a theropod is quite small. Meat is easily digested.

Tendons

Teeth
The teeth of a theropod are sharp and finely serrated like steak knives. Often the jaws work with a back-and-forward action so that the upper and lower teeth produce a saw-like effect.

Feet
With three functioning toes.

much food to fuel its system than does a cold-blooded animal of the same size. So, a cold-blooded, meat-eating dinosaur could make one kill, eat as much as it wanted, and then rest for weeks, like a modern python. However, a warm-blooded, meat-eating dinosaur would have to hunt nearly all the time. Warm-blooded animals also need insulation to regulate their body temperature. In mammals this is formed from hair, while in birds it is formed from feathers. We have evidence that some of the later meat-eating dinosaurs were covered in hair or feathers. Lake deposits at Liaoning have fossils that show this, and skeletons of some of the ostrich-mimic (ornithomimid) dinosaurs have pores along the arm bones that indicate where feathers were attached. They are all small, late dinosaurs, from the Cretaceous period, but we do not know how far back they had these features. Big dinosaurs, even if they were warm blooded, would not need as much insulation – a modern elephant, for example, has very little hair.

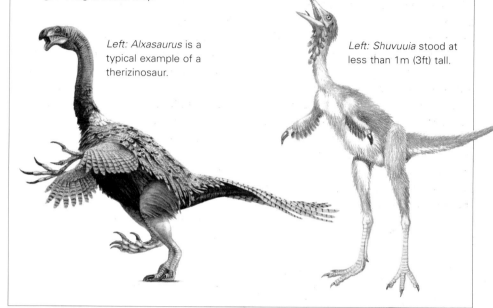

Therizinosaurs

The therizinosaurs are a side-group of the theropod family. They had heads that looked more like the heads of plant-eaters, and the hip bone was similar in shape to a bird's. The hands were armed with powerful claws, probably used for food gathering in some way.

Left: Alxasaurus is a typical example of a therizinosaur.

Alvarezsaurids

The alvarezsaurids, such as *Shuvuuia*, were a group of small, bird-like theropods. They had remarkable forearms, which were stunted and carried a single big claw. The arms looked like atrophied wings but their purpose is still a mystery.

Left: Shuvuuia stood at less than 1m (3ft) tall.

Skin covering *Usually scaly, but sometimes feathered in small types of dinosaur.*

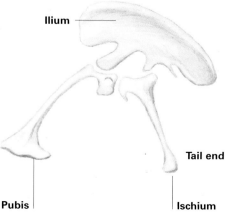

Hip socket

Ilium

Tail end

Pubis

Ischium

Hip *(left) A theropod meat-eater had the saurischian hip – with the arrangement of bones like those of a lizard. At each side there was a top bone called the ilium, which held the leg muscles. Pointing forward and down from the hip socket was the pubis, which took the weight of the animal as it lies down. Sweeping down and back was the ischium, to which the tail muscles and the inside leg muscles were attached.*

Skull *(above) A dinosaur's skull is a lightly-built framework of struts of bone. The teeth constantly grow and drop out, each one being replaced by another that is growing beneath it.*

SAUROPODS AND PROSAUROPODS

The sauropods were the big plant-eaters of dinosaur times, with heavy elephantine bodies, long necks and whip-like tails. They evolved from the prosauropods in the late Triassic period and became the main plant-eaters of Jurassic times. They existed until the end of the Cretaceous period.

The only obvious resemblance between a sauropod and its theropod relative was in the arrangement of the hip bones. They both had hips like a lizard's, with the pubis bone pointing down and forward. As with meat-eaters, the innards had to be carried forward of this pubis bone, and since the sauropods had huge, plant-digesting intestines, these innards tended to be very heavy. Since the heavy body in front of the hips made it very difficult for the animal to balance on its hind legs, sauropods were nearly always four-footed. The front legs were usually shorter than the hind legs, suggesting that their ancestors were two-footed. The neck was particularly long and carried a small head. The tail was very long and often ended in a fine whip point that may have been used as a weapon.

There is a great deal of controversy about whether the sauropods were warm- or cold-blooded. The argument for warm-bloodedness is their close-ness to the theropod line, some of which were definitely warm-blooded. On the other hand the sheer size of the animal – a beast weighing tens of tonnes would be able to conserve its heat more easily than a small animal, and would not need a warm-blooded metabolism. Then there was the problem of being able to eat enough food through the little jaws to fuel a warm-blooded lifestyle. A compromise theory suggests that what we regard as warm-blooded and cold-blooded are really just the extreme ends of a graded sequence. It may be that the theropods lay close to the warm-blooded end, and the sauropods close to the cold-blooded end. In any case it is unlikely that the sauropods would have been covered in feathers or hair.

Above: The skin impression left by a sauropod shows a relatively smooth skin covered by scales.

Liver

Large intestine

Ligament
Supporting the weight of the neck.

Circulation system
The heart of a sauropod had to be particularly powerful to pump blood from one end to the other, and to send it up to the heights reached by the neck. It has been suggested that there may have been several hearts along the length of the neck to help the circulation.

Gizzard
The digestive system is much bigger than that of a meat-eater's. The lack of chewing ability meant that sauropods swallowed stones frequently, and these stones gathered in a gizzard to grind up the food as it entered the digestive system. Modern plant-eating birds, such as turkeys or pheasants, also do this since they cannot chew with their beaks.

Caeca
Sac-shaped intestine extensions.

Small intestine

There is also some dispute as to what did cover the sauropods. Conventional restorations show a wrinkled, elephant-like skin. Isolated remains, however, indicate the possibility of a scaly skin like a lizard's, and even horny spikes down the back. These issues are still disputed.

Prosauropod teeth

The teeth of a prosauropod were leaf-shaped, overlapping and coarsely serrated, like vegetable shredders. They had evolved to rip up coarse plant material. In comparison those of the later sauropods were quite simple.

The teeth of a sauropod were arranged for raking and combing rather than for chewing. Some dinosaurs, such as Diplodocus, *had peg-like teeth, while others like* Camarasaurus, *had teeth that were spoon-shaped. A feature of the jaw bone is the low position of the joint. As in most plant-eating dinosaurs, this allowed for good leverage to break off tough food.*

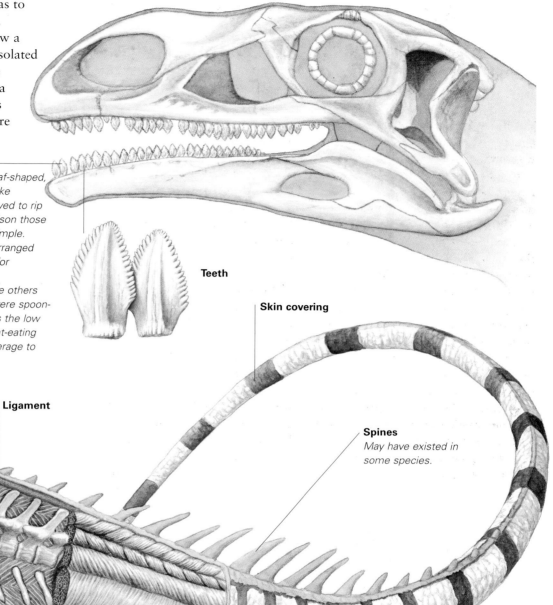

Teeth

Skin covering

Ligament

Spines
May have existed in some species.

Cloaca

Gristle
Wedge to take the animal's weight.

Prosauropods

The prosauropods were early relatives of the sauropods, and may have been their ancestors. It used to be thought that they formed a link between the meat-eaters and the plant-eaters, being able to take both plant and animal food. Modern studies show that their teeth were purely for plant-eating, and their jaws had a low hinge like that of the later sauropods. Early forms were lightweight, two-footed animals, but some of the later prosauropods were big and four-footed, like true sauropods.

Above: Effrasia *is a typical early prosauropod.*

ORNITHOPODS

The second major group of dinosaurs were those with hip bones arranged like those of a bird, with the pubis bone swept back. They evolved into a number of different lines, including the armoured and horned types, but the basic anatomy is seen in the two-footed plant-eating types – the ornithopods.

Ornithopods were all plant-eaters. The basic "bird-hipped" dinosaur type was the two-footed plant-eater. Examples ranged from small, chicken-sized animals up to monsters 15m (50ft) long or more.

An ornithopod, being a plant eater, had a large, complex, digestive system. This was carried well back, beneath the hips – the new arrangement of hip bones allowed for this. That meant that this animal, even though it was a plant-eater with heavy intestines, could still walk on its hind legs, balanced by a heavy tail, just like the theropods.

From a distance, a lightweight ornithopod may have looked like a theropod, but there were certain differences. For one thing the body of the plant-eater was much bigger, giving it a pot-bellied appearance. Then there were the hands. A theropod had no more than three fingers on the hand, whereas the ornithopod had the full complement of five. The head was also quite different. The jaw had a chewing system that was different from that of any other dinosaur seen so far.

The ornithopods evolved early in the age of dinosaurs, but for the Triassic and Jurassic periods were mostly quite small animals. The long-necked sauropods were the big plant-eaters of this time. Then, in the

Fleshy crest known from some duckbills

Prepubis

Ilium

Hollow nasal tubes, forming crest

Duck-like bill

Skull *(below): The upper teeth were attached to bones that were loosely articulated with the rest of the skull, allowing an efficient grinding action.*

Skull bones

Grinding surface of teeth

Upper jaw moving outwards

Cheeks

Lower jaw moving upwards

Weight-bearing pad on forefeet

Large plant-digesting gut

Fingers

Cretaceous, they blossomed. They spread everywhere, at the expense of the sauropods, and some attained great size. The biggest ones became too heavy to spend much time on their hind legs and so they moved about on all fours (as youngsters they still scampered around as two-footed animals).

The ornithopod head was totally different from that of the other dinosaurs. The jaws had batteries of grinding teeth, usually with wrinkled enamel, and they were constantly replaced to ensure that there was always a grinding surface. In the advanced forms the upper jaws

were fitted loosely into the skull. This meant that as the lower jaw came upwards, the upper jaw moved outwards so that the sloping surfaces on the upper and lower teeth ripped past one another, producing the grinding action. The fact that the rows of teeth were set in from the side of the skull shows that these animals had cheeks. The cheeks formed pouches that held the food as it was being ground. A sharp beak at the front of the mouth, supported by a bone that the theropods and sauropods did not possess, created an efficient, food-gathering mouth. With such a complex chewing mechanism there was no need for stomach stones to aid digestion. The armoured and horned dinosaurs also had these features.

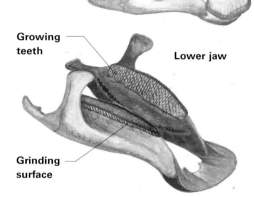

Hollow nasal tubes, forming crest

Growing teeth

Lower jaw

Grinding surface

Teeth (above): Although the teeth of a duckbill numbered many hundred, only a few of them were working at any one time. They were tightly-packed, like dates in a box, and continually growing. Those at the grinding edge were constantly being worn away and replaced by those growing from below.

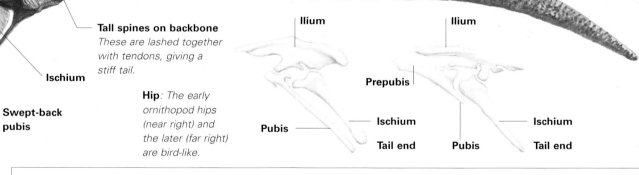

Tall spines on backbone
These are lashed together with tendons, giving a stiff tail.

Ischium

Swept-back pubis

Hip: The early ornithopod hips (near right) and the later (far right) are bird-like.

Ilium

Pubis

Ischium

Tail end

Ilium

Prepubis

Pubis

Ischium

Tail end

Hypsilophodon
A typical small ornithopod. Its plump body was supported on its hind legs, balanced by the tail. Its head had the chewing teeth, the cheeks and the beak. Its long hind legs show that this was a running animal, able to flee from danger.

Below: Hypsilophodon.

Ouranosaurus
One of the larger ornithopods. It is so heavy that it spent most of its time on all fours. A tall array of spines along its back may have supported a sail, or some kind of fatty hump for use as a food store, like a modern camel.

Below: Ouranosaurus.

Tenontosaurus
A particularly common dinosaur on the early Cretaceous plains of North America. It was intermediate in size between *Hypsilophodon* and *Ouranosaurus*, and had a particularly long tail.

Below: Tenontosaurus.

ARMOURED DINOSAURS

The basic ornithopod dinosaur, with a heavy plant-eating body and bird-shaped hips was the shape from which the armoured dinosaurs developed. The stegosaurs had plates, the ankylosaurs had armour, and the ceratopsians had horns.

Three groups of dinosaurs developed from the basic ornithopod pattern, all bearing armour of one kind or another: these were the stegosaurs, ankylosaurs and ceratopsians. Various lines of ornithischian dinosaur developed armour and, because of the added weight, reverted from the two-footed ornithopod-like stance to a four-footed mode of life. The first of these to evolve were the stegosaurs, in which the armour consisted of a double row of plates and spines. Later came the ankylosaurs, with armour that formed a mosaic across the back. Last to appear were the ceratopsians, where the armour was confined to the head.

Stegosaurs

The stegosaurs, or the plated dinosaurs, are found in Jurassic and early Cretaceous times. They had plates that ran down their backs, and often spines on the tail. These tail spines were used as weapons when swung at an attacker. Sometimes there were spines on the shoulder as well.

There has always been disagreement regarding the function of the

Left: With spines on the back and neck, plates down the tail, and an armoured shield across the lower back Polacanthus was one of the more lightly armoured ankylosaurs.

plates. The traditional view is that they were a defence mechanism, no doubt being covered in horn, and probably had pointed corners and sharp edges. They protected the backbone from an attack by a tall predator, but that meant the flanks were unprotected. A second theory is that the plates were part of a heat-exchange mechanism. If they were covered in skin rich in blood vessels, they would absorb the sun's warmth in the morning and shed heat with the midday wind. This seems an attractive theory to explain

the broad plates like those of *Stegosaurus*, but it is not so logical when dealing with the narrower plates of the smaller and more primitive forms like *Kentrosaurus*.

Ankylosaurs

The ankylosaurs developed in Cretaceous times, as the stegosaurs declined. They were the armoured dinosaurs, with the armour formed from bony studs set in the skin and covered in horn.

There were several different types of ankylosaur. Some, such as *Polacanthus*, had a thick rigid mosaic of tiny studs over the hips and spines sticking out at the side. Others, such as *Edmontonia*, had a fierce array of spikes sticking sideways and forward from the shoulders. Others, such as *Euoplocephalus*,

Right: The broad plates of Stegosaurus would have been brightly coloured for signalling.

Right: The plates of Kentrosaurus were smaller and less prominent.

Right: Edmontonia *was an ankylosaur with defensive spines on its shoulders.*

Below: Euoplocephalus *had armour in plates all over the head, back and down the tail, finishing with a massive tail club.*

had the defence concentrated around the tail where the bones at the tip were fused into a monstrous club, and the tail vertebrae were fused together to make a rigid shaft.

The ankylosaurs had very stout bodies that contained very sophisticated digestive systems. Probably like modern cows they carried fermenting guts to allow bacterial action to break down tough plant material before it could be fully digested.

Ceratopsians

The last dinosaur group to evolve was the ceratopsians, or the horned dinosaurs. Ceratopsians were distinguished by having all their armour on their heads. It may be that the head armour evolved from ridges at the back of the skull. The ridges anchored the very strong jaw muscles which these animals needed to chew the tough cycad fronds on which they fed. *Psittacosaurus* was typical of these early ceratopsians. All these dinosaurs had the same beak and cheek arrangement as the ornithopods. However, in the ceratopsians, the teeth were evolved for chopping rather than for chewing.

The most spectacular ceratopsians, like *Triceratops*, lived at the end of the Cretaceous period, when herds of them roamed the plains of North America. Each kind had a different set of horns and a different neck shield, allowing them to tell each other apart.

A side-branch of the ceratopsian family was a group we call the boneheads. Their armour consisted of a solid dome of bone on top of the skull, possibly covered in horn. They were mostly quite small goat-sized animals, such as *Tylocephale*, but others, such as *Pachycephalosaurus*, grew to the size of its *Triceratops* cousin.

Below: *The armoured neck shields of ceratopsians like* Chasmosaurus *were for signalling as well as defence. They would have been brightly-coloured like flags.*

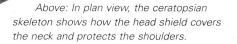

Above: *In plan view, the ceratopsian skeleton shows how the head shield covers the neck and protects the shoulders.*

COPROLITES AND DIET

We have plenty of information that shows what the dinosaurs ate and how they ate it. The evidence includes close examination of their fossilized jaws and teeth, fossilized stomach contents and also of fossil dung, known as coprolites.

We know that the carnivorous theropods had a particular kind of tooth and jaw apparatus for shearing meat. The teeth of sauropods were designed for raking leaves from trees. The teeth and jaws of ornithopods and the armoured dinosaurs were built for chewing, chopping and munching, and processing plant food before swallowing it. Teeth and jaws represent physical evidence of the type of diet that the dinosaurs had. But there are other lines of investigation.

Palaeontologists describe fossil dung as "coprolite". A coprolite can be a very valuable tool to work out the diet of something that is dead and fossilized. Dinosaur coprolites are rare. Most coprolites we find come from marine animals, such as fish. As with all other fossils, marine conditions provide a far better preservation medium than any land habitat. A piece of dung deposited on land will be trampled on, decomposed or eaten by bacteria, fungi or other organisms. In fact, one of the ways of identifying a structure as a coprolite of a land-living animal is by the presence of dung-beetle burrows through it. Dung is a remarkably nutritious substance to certain creatures. Yet for all that, there have

Above: A Tyrannosaurus *upper jaw.*

been a fair number of dinosaur coprolites discovered, and they give a good insight into their diets.

Theropod coprolites seem to be more common than those of plant-eating dinosaurs. This is probably because they contain a high proportion of bone material that makes them more robust than the stuff produced by a plant-eater. Studies have been done to try to determine what that bone material might be. The chemistry of a coprolite reflects the chemistry of the meal, and chemical studies on coprolites from a *Tyrannosaurus* or one of its relatives suggest a diet predominantly of duckbilled ornithopods.

The coprolites of herbivorous dinosaurs are more problematic. They are very difficult to identify and, when they are found, it is almost impossible to determine what dinosaur produced them. Coprolites in Jurassic rocks in Yorkshire, England, are identified as dinosaur droppings simply because of their size – no other plant-eating animals about at that time could produce such a volume of dung. These coprolites consist of a mass of pellets like deer droppings, and contain the

partly digested remains of cycad-like plants. Coprolites have been found close to duckbill nesting sites in Montana, and they contain shredded conifer stem material. Duckbills had powerful enough teeth to allow them to chew woody twigs to extract the nourishment. Grass structures in sauropod coprolites from India show that grass existed in late Cretaceous times, much earlier than first thought.

Below: Some dinosaurs swallowed stomach stones to help grind up food once in the stomach. These polished stones would have been regurgitated and swapped for stones with a sharper edge.

Below: Fossilized dung, shaped like huge droppings, can provide a wealth of information about what dinosaurs ate.

Cololites are similar to coprolites. These are fossilized stomach contents that we are sometimes lucky enough to find in the body cavity of a fully preserved dinosaur skeleton. The best examples of stomach contents are those that consist of a meal that has not been digested. The excellent skeleton of *Compsognathus* found in the lagoonal limestones of Solnhöfen, in southern Germany, contains the bones of a little lizard in its stomach area, its last meal. The skeleton of one of the *Coelophysis* that died of hunger as a water hole dried up contains the bones of a small crocodile.

Most cololites are in less good condition. A cololite found in the skeleton of the Australian ankylosaur *Minmi* contains the seeds of flowering plants and the spores of ferns. The concentration of seeds suggests that the ankylosaur went for those in particular, and may have been important in spreading the seeds around through its faeces. The chopped up state of the material indicates that it had been well chewed

Right: In extreme times dinosaurs are known to have eaten their own young in an attempt to survive, as observed in Majungotholus.

before being swallowed, more proof that these animals had cheeks. Furthermore, a cololite from a duckbill in Montana has spores in the stomach part that come from plants different from those in its intestine. This suggests that the animal moved about as it ate.

Some stomach contents consist of the stomach stones swallowed by sauropods. In the flood plain

Below: The tiny bones in the stomach of this Coelophysis are those of a crocodile. They were once thought to have been remains of its own young.

deposits of the North American Jurassic Morrison Formation there are little heaps of polished stones. They have been identified as stomach stones that became too worn and smooth to be of use. The animal vomited them up and replaced them with sharper stones.

More indirect evidence of diet comes from tooth marks. *Allosaurus* teeth marks have been found on the bones of Jurassic sauropods. Broken and shed *Allosaurus* teeth have also even been found near such remains. Marks that match *Tyrannosaurus* teeth have been found on the bones of *Triceratops*.

And *Tyrannosaurus* teeth have even been found wedged in the bones of duckbilled *Hypacrosaurus*. There can hardly be better indications of feeding behaviour.

DINOSAUR FOOTPRINTS

*Footprints are the best tools we have to tell how an animal lived. The study of footprints is known
as ichnology, and the study of fossil footprints, is known as palaeoichnology. The science involves an
understanding of how sediments and animals behave.*

A dead dinosaur may have left a skeleton, but in all likelihood there will only be a few bones left for us to study once the rest of it has been eaten or eroded. It is even more likely that there will be no surviving physical remains. At best, there can only be one skeleton. However, that single animal will have made millions of footprints during its lifetime, and these footprints, if preserved, can tell us all sorts of things about the animal's lifestyle.

The specialist study of fossil footprints is known as palaeo-ichnology. It has a long pedigree. In the early nineteenth century, three-toed fossil footprints were found in the Triassic sandstones of Connecticut, USA. They were studied by local naturalist Edward Hitchcock, who thought they were the footprints of giant birds (there was no concept of dinosaurs at that time). Even today it is almost impossible to match a footprint to the animal that made it. Palaeoichnologists overcome this problem by attributing 'ichnospecies' names to them. This allows each footprint or footprint track to be catalogued and studied without

Above and right: Fossil footprints can tell us whether an animal travelled alone or in groups, whether there were different sizes of animal passing by and the speed at which the animal travelled. Here are several Apatosaurus *trackways from the Morrison Formation, USA.*

referring to the animal that may have made it. The name of an ichnospecies often ends with the suffix *opus*. For example, *Anomoepus* is a footprint that may or may not have been made by a small ornithopod, *Tetrasauropus* is a footprint that was probably made by a prosauropod, and *Brontopodus* is almost certainly the footprint of a big sauropod, but which one? Most footprints are so vague that we can only tell that an animal of some kind passed this way.

If we find a series of footprints (or a trackway), made as the animal was moving along, we can tell if it had been travelling alone, in a pair, or in a larger group. Sometimes we find different sizes of the same kind of footprint, indicating that a family group of old and young had passed. Some trackways can be traced over tens or hundreds of kilometres, usually in separate outcrops. They are known as megatracksites.

Below: Three-toed theropod footprints found in early Jurassic rocks in Spain.

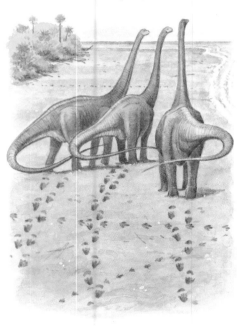

Below: A true print in the top layer usually has the mud squeezed up around it, and may preserve the skin texture of the foot.

Dinosaur trackways

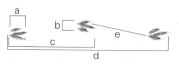

The dimensions measured when studying fossil tracks are:
- Foot length (a).
- Foot width (b).
- Step length (the distance between successive prints) (c).
- Stride length (the distance between successive prints made by the same foot) (d).
- Pace angulation (the angle between three successive prints) (e).
- Angle of rotation (the angle that the direction of the foot makes with the direction of travel).
- Various equations using these parameters can be used to estimate a dinosaur's speed.

Below and left: Paleoichnology can be a highly mathematical science. Using the values measured here, and the dimensions of a dinosaur's leg (if known), we can calculate its walking speed.

However, gauging the size of the footprint can be tricky. The print that fossilized in the rock may not be the actual print impressed by the dinosaur's foot. When an animal leaves a footprint in the top layer of sediment, another less distinct print is impressed into the layer beneath. Often the top layer is washed off and only the impression in the lower layer (the underprint) is preserved. It is essential to recognize underprints so that we do not make erroneous measurements; they tend to be smaller than true footprints and, if confused, would make calculations of speed unreliable. Fortunately, a true print can usually be recognized by its detail. If we find a print that actually preserves the skin

Below: Many prints are preserved as casts. A footprint may be filled by later sediments, and when these sediments become rock they preserve a three-dimensional impression of the print that stands proud of the bedding plane.

texture of the underside of the foot, then we can be confident that we are looking at a true print.

Trackways

Sometimes, tracks can be so spectacular that it is easy to jump to unwarranted interpretations in the excitement of discovery. A track that was clearly made by a herd of sauropods may have a theropod track running parallel to it. This would appear to show a sauropod herd being stalked by a theropod that is waiting to attack. Or the theropod may have followed the same route days later – it is difficult to tell. And a track of sauropod footprints that only show the tips of the front toes and nothing else, may be interpreted as the marks made by the animal swimming and poling

Below: The shapes of footprints can be misleading. The very long print (top), was made in soft mud, where the toes dragged a blob of mud along (bottom).

Left: Footprint in top layer of earth.

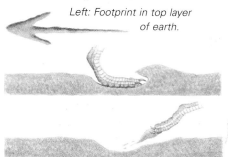

itself through the water using its front feet. More likely it is a set of underprints, with the narrower front feet penetrating deeper into the sediment and forming underprints, while the broader hind feet spread the weight and remain on the surface.

Below top: A dinosaur makes a footprint, with the true print impressed into the top layer of sediment and an underprint pressed into the layer below.

Below middle: The top layer of sediment is washed away.

Below bottom: Only the underprint is preserved.

DINOSAUR EGGS

We know that dinosaurs reproduced by laying eggs. However it is difficult to match the fossil eggs found with a particular species of dinosaur – the first dinosaur eggs were misidentified for 70 years. The study of these fossils show that dinosaurs laid eggs that were more like those of birds than of other reptiles.

It has always been assumed that dinosaurs laid eggs, as other large reptiles do. However, it was in the 1920s that the first dinosaur eggs were actually found. A series of expeditions into the Gobi Desert, led by Roy Chapman Andrews of the American Museum of Natural History, USA, uncovered several nests containing eggs and a large number of skeletons of the ceratopsian *Protoceratops*. For 70 years these "*Protoceratops* eggs" were the most famous and important dinosaur eggs found. At the site, the structure of the nest, the arrangement of eggs within it, and the proximity of the nests to one another were all clearly visible. It was suggested that there was evidence that the nests had been attacked. A small theropod named *Oviraptor*, or egg-stealer, was found close to one of the nests, having been overwhelmed by a sandstorm while trying to rob it. Then, in the 1980s, more of the same nests were found, again by an expedition from the American Museum of Natural History, but this time one of the nests had the skeleton of an *Oviraptor* actually sitting on it. The nests and eggs are now believed to be those of the *Oviraptor*.

Above: Sauropod eggs are almost spherical in shape.

At another site known as Egg Mountain in Montana, USA, nests with eggs and remains of the ornithopod *Orodromeus* were found, with remains of the theropod *Troodon*. The *Troodon* was first believed to be at the site intending to rob the nests, but the nests are now believed to be those of the *Troodon*. The *Orodromeus* remains are thought to be from corpses that the parent theropods had brought back to feed their young. The provenance of the *Troodon* eggs was confirmed when some of the eggs were dissected and baby *Troodon* were found inside. However it is unusual to be able to dissect a dinosaur egg. A fossilized egg is an egg that died before it had a chance to hatch. When the egg dies the embryo inside is usually destroyed. Beetles burrow through the shell and lay eggs, and when the larvae

Left: There are skeletons of Oviraptor *parents, in Mongolia, actually lying over their eggs in the nest, their wings spread out over them to keep them warm while they incubated.*

Left and right: Skeletons of baby Troodon have been found inside eggs. As in other animals, the babies have proportionally larger heads and feet than the adults.

hatch they eat the dinosaur egg's contents. Most fossilized eggs contain only scraps of bone that are so jumbled that they are unidentifiable.

Shell fragments are often found associated with nesting sites, where the eggs came to maturity and hatched. Modern microscopy techniques have been used on shell fragments so that dinosaur egg shells can be compared with those of modern animals. It was once assumed that dinosaur eggs had soft or flexible shells, like modern reptiles. However, study of the crystalline structure of fossil egg shells shows that the majority of them were hard and rigid, like those of birds.

Egg identification

As with footprints, it is difficult to assign a fossil egg to a dinosaur species, and it can only be successfully accomplished in rare occurrences when an identifiable embryo can be found inside the egg, or if a nest has the skeleton of a parent nearby.

The south German Solnhöfen skeleton of *Compsognathus* has a number of spherical objects associated with it. They are thought to be unlaid eggs that burst out of the body cavity after the animal died. Such an association of eggs and skeleton is very rare, though.

As with footprints, palaeontologists give names to particular fossil eggs – names that do not imply

Above: Maiasaura *nests show all stages of nesting behaviour – complete eggs, broken eggshell, bones of hatchlings and skeletons of well-grown youngsters that have not yet left the nest.*

identification of the egg layer. Such a classification is an "oospecies".

Most dinosaur eggs are found in nests. Occasionally they look as if they have been laid in holes in the ground without much preparation – a spiral of eggs found in France is thought to have been laid by a stegosaur that just deposited them and left. Most of the nests that we know about are quite complex structures, and are found together in rookeries or nesting sites. The nests laid by the duckbill ornithopod *Maiasaura* in Montana are the best studied. A typical nest consists of a mount of mud or soil, with a depression in the top. That depression is filled with ferns

Above: Ornamentation on the fossil shell surface as well as the crystal structure of the eggshell itself help palaeontologists to identify oospecies.

and twigs, providing insulation for the eggs that are laid inside it. Each nest is positioned about an adult dinosaur length from the next, so that they do not disturb one another.

Right: Egg nests have been found in Montana, USA, at a site known as Egg Mountain.

DINOSAUR BABIES AND FAMILY LIFE

Fossils found at nesting sites can tell us how quickly dinosaurs grew, for example, by looking at the structure of the individual bones and analyzing their growth lines. We can also tell that growing dinosaurs were subject to diseases and injuries throughout life.

The *Maiasaura* nests in Montana, USA, have been the subject of the most studies on dinosaur family life. The Montana nesting site was by a lake in the uplands. Besides nesting behaviour, this site also provided all sorts of information about how the animals lived and grew. Once out of the egg, a baby *Maiasaura* was a small, vulnerable animal, about 45cm (18in) long. It remained in the nest and was nurtured by its parents, who brought food in the form of leaves and fruits to the nest. Nests were protected against raids by large lizards and theropod dinosaurs, such as *Troodon*. Seasonal climates meant that once in a while the *Maiasaura* herd had to leave the upland nesting site and migrate to the coastal plains, where food was still plentiful. The nestling grew to twice its birth length in about five months. At this juvenile stage the young dinosaur

Below: The quite recent find of a parent Psittacosaurus *with 34 young demonstrates that some dinosaurs did nurture their young in the nest.*

Above: Evidence suggests that some genera of dinosaurs looked after their young, nurturing the hatchlings and bringing back food until they were five months old.

would have left the nest, and followed the parents, learning how to find food for itself. Juveniles continued to grow, and after about a year reached a length of about 3.5m (11½ft).

The microscopic structure of the bones show us that the full adult length of about 7m (23ft) was reached in about six years, after which time the growth rate became very much slower. The conclusion is that dinosaurs, or at least duckbill dinosaurs, grew extremely quickly in the early part of their lives, and that the growth rate then slowed. This is the same growth pattern that we see in modern mammals and birds, but not in reptiles. The *Maiasaura* herds returned to their nesting area when it was time to breed, a round trip of around 300km (185 miles).

Sauropods

Similar evidence for the family life of sauropod dinosaurs comes from a site called Auca Mahuevo, in Argentina. This late Cretaceous site has a vast array of nests from a titanosaurid sauropod, probably *Saltasaurus*, made on a flood plain. During the breeding season herds of pregnant females descended on the area – a region that was just out of reach of most floodwaters from nearby streams. Their nests were simple compared with the nest structures of *Maiasaura* – they merely scooped out a shallow basin, about 1m (3ft) in diameter, with their clawed front feet, and laid their eggs in this. Each female laid 15–40 eggs in nests positioned 1.5–5m (5–16½ft) apart. Having laid their eggs, the females abandoned them, without any intention of looking after the nestlings once they hatched. It is possible that they remained in the area to discourage the big meat-eating dinosaurs, such as *Aucasaurus*, that roamed the area.

Below: Young Maiasaura *left their nests after about five months of growing and being tended by their parents.*

The young sauropods, on hatching, would have been about 30cm (12in) long – little animals compared with the adults who were 30 times their length – but they were equipped to find their own food immediately. Youngsters able to look after themselves immediately, are known as "precocious hatchlings" by biologists, and this is true of most reptiles today. Once out of the nest, the perils of the outside world awaited the young dinosaurs.

Dinosaur remains have been found showing signs of sickness and injury that would have prevented many from reaching old age. Palaeopathology, the study of ancient diseases, has shown that a range of traumas and diseases afflicted the dinosaurs.

Many ceratopsian skeletons have healed fractures to their rib-cages, suggesting injuries due to fighting. One ceratopsian skull has been found with a hole in it that matches the dimensions of a ceratopsian horn,

Above: As Maiasaura *youngsters grew, they joined the herd in their annual migrations to the productive feeding grounds.*

suggesting a head-on fight between the two animals. Tyrannosaurs suffered from gout. There are at least two examples of this disease that would have been brought on by a surfeit of red meat in the diet. Arthritis has also been identified in quite a few dinosaurs, including *Iguanodon*, where foot bones have been fused together. Additionally, a number of the bigger ornithopods have fractures to the upward-projecting spines from the tail vertebrae close to the hips. It has been suggested that these breakages were caused by excessive violence during mating.

DEATH AND TAPHONOMY

The study of what happens to a body between its death and its fossilization is known as taphonomy. The taphonomy of an individual fossil organism is extremely important to the scientist who wishes to find out about that animal, and the conditions under which it lived and died.

Fossil-bearing rocks are usually full of bivalves, or sea urchins, or corals, or even fish. Fossils of sea-living things are common because when they die, creatures that live in the sea are likely to sink to the bottom and be covered by sand, mud and other marine sediments. As these sediments solidify, the dead creatures become fossils. An animal that lives and dies on land, on the other hand, may have been killed by a hunting animal and may be eaten on the spot. Once the hunter has eaten its fill, scavenging animals will take

their pick of the prey. The bones are broken up and carried away, and what is left is eaten by insects and broken down by fungi and bacteria. After a few weeks there is nothing left of the dead animal but a smear on the ground – certainly nothing left to fossilize.

The vast majority of dinosaurs have left nothing to tell us of their existence. However if a dinosaur's body falls into a river and is buried in flood deposits, or if it dies in a toxic lake where no scavengers can live, or if it is engulfed

and buried in a sandstorm, there is a chance that the remains will survive in fossil form.

Fossil finds

Dinosaur fossils are found in a number of forms. The most spectacular is the "articulated skeleton". This is the ultimate prize because it has all the bones still joined together as when the dinosaur died. However, the temptation is to leave it as found, and so information is lost if the skeleton is not dissected and studied minutely.

The fate of a *Stegosaurus*

A dinosaur skeleton is rarely found complete. Many things can have happened to the dead body before it became buried and fossilized.

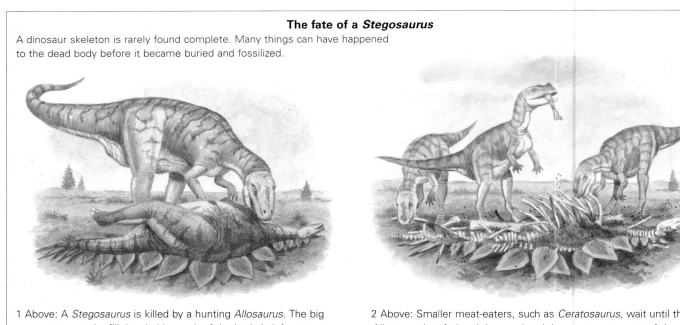

1 Above: A *Stegosaurus* is killed by a hunting *Allosaurus*. The big meat-eater eats its fill. Inevitably much of the body is left uneaten.

2 Above: Smaller meat-eaters, such as *Ceratosaurus*, wait until the *Allosaurus* has fed and departed and then scavenge most of the flesh left behind.

3 Above: The scraps that remain are eaten by even smaller scavengers, and the rest is broken down by insects and fungi. By this time the skeleton is scattered.

4 Above: Eventually the scattered bones are buried by river deposits during the wet season as the plain floods. Now the process of fossilization can begin.

Above: The skin impression of a Hadrosaur *was created as mud solidified around a corpse before it decayed – a rare occurence.*

The next best thing is an "associated skeleton". This is a jumble of bones that obviously comes from the same animal, but which have been broken up and scattered. Usually something is missing, carried away by the forces that pulled it apart. More common is an "isolated bone". Sometimes its origin is obvious, but not always, and scientific errors have been perpetrated by the misidentification of isolated bones. *Dravidosaurus* was thought to be a stegosaur, living in India where no

Below: A partly excavated isolated femur (thigh bone) that belonged to a sauropod dinosaur, preserved in Upper Jurassic redbed mudstones of the Upper Shaximiao Formation, in Sichuan, China.

Above: The associated skeleton of a sauropod in Jurassic sediment in the Dinosaur National Monument, Utah, USA.

other stegosaurs had been found, and existing tens of millions of years after the stegosaurs were supposed to have died out. The isolated bones on which the identification was based were actually parts of a plesiosaur, a marine reptile.

Bits of bone that have no scientific value whatsoever are termed "float". Some dinosaur excavations map and catalogue every bit of float found, in the hope that they might one day yield some information. Most excavations just ignore them.

Finally there are trace fossils, footprints, droppings, eggs and other lines of evidence that a dinosaur existed, but without any physical remains. Paradoxically it may be that trace fossils tell us more about the animal's life than the body fossils.

Below: An articulated skeleton of Lambeosaurus *where the components have been kept together as in life.*

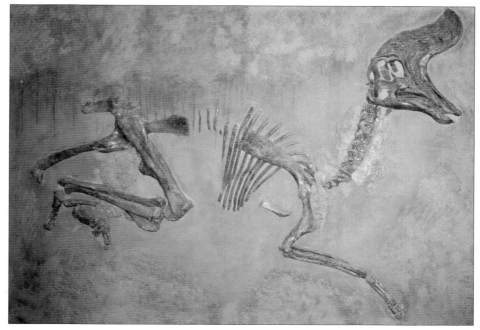

DESERTS AND ARID HABITATS

We often associate dinosaur remains with water, and animals living near it are more likely to be buried in sediment once they have died than those that lived far away from it. However, there are a number of occurrences where dinosaurs of very dry habitats have been found fossilized.

The Gobi Desert was a desert even in Cretaceous times. Ephemeral lakes surrounded by plains of scrubby vegetation were separated by vast areas of shifting sand dunes. Here roamed herds of the small ceratopsian *Protoceratops*, in such numbers that one palaeontologist dubbed them 'the sheep of the Cretaceous period'. Occasionally, the harsh, dry winds of the desert overwhelmed these herds in a sandstorm or a dust storm, and sometimes they were engulfed by sliding sand as an unstable dune collapsed. Either occurrence had the effect of killing the animals where they stood, and preserving them in a tomb of dry sand that eventually solidified into desert sandstone.

A specimen that shows just how quickly such an event occurred was found in the 1970s. The skeletons of a *Protoceratops* and a fierce little *Velociraptor* where found wrapped around one another. The meat-eater's arm was seized in the ceratopsian's beak, while the long claws of the former were clutched tightly to the latter's head shield. The two had been buried and died while in the middle of their struggle. Elsewhere in the desert, dinosaur nests and eggs have been preserved in sandstone. One nest, belonging to the theropod *Oviraptor*, even had the mother dinosaur sitting across it, in a vain attempt to incubate her eggs as the sandstorm swept down and engulfed her.

In the Triassic period, back at the beginning of the Age of Dinosaurs and a whole supercontinent away from the Gobi Desert, southern England consisted of an arid, limestone plateau where more fossils have been found. Early prosauropods, such as *Thecodontosaurus*, eked out a living here on the scrappy vegetation. The plateau was riddled with gullies and caves, and moist underground air seeped to the surface producing a slightly lusher vegetation at the cave mouths. Plant-eaters were

Below: The shifting sands and airborne dust clouds of the desert were constant threats to the dinosaurs of the late Cretaceous Gobi Desert. Often they were buried in hollows or on the flanks of collapsing sand dunes.

tempted to these areas, and occasionally lost their footing and fell to their deaths. There they were devoured by cave-dwelling animals, or lay until they were covered by cave debris and fossilized. This leads us to the anomaly in which Triassic dinosaur remains are found in much older Carboniferous rocks. The Carboniferous limestones formed the uplands and the Triassic animals were fossilized in them.

We can often tell if a dinosaur died in an arid environment. As a dead body dries out in the heat, the tendons that link the bones shrink. In most dinosaurs tendons lash together the bones of the backbone and help to support the weight of the neck and tail. When these tendons dry and

contract, they pull the tail upwards and the neck backwards, drawing the skull over the shoulders and back. An articulated skeleton found in this position shows that the body dried out before burial. Many articulated skeletons are found like this.

Above: A sandstorm could mean death for a large animal like a dinosaur. It could also mean that its skeleton was preserved entirely and articulated. An animal engulfed in tonnes of sand suffocated quickly, but the sheer weight of the sediment kept it in place and once the soft tissues decayed the bones remained undisturbed.

Below: An arid limestone plateau habitat is the setting for a swallowhole into which lizards and a Thecodontosaurus have fallen. Eventually the swallowhole is filled with debris and the bones of the dead animals fossilize.

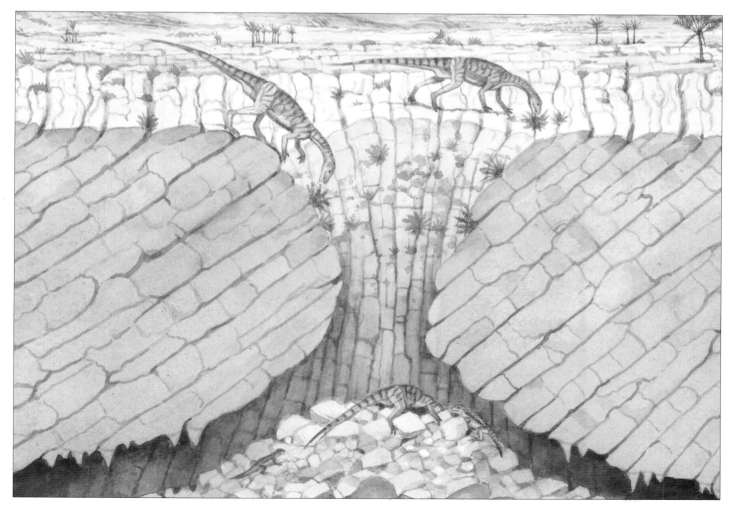

OASES AND DESERT STREAMS

In an arid landscape, the presence of water is a great attraction to life. Where desert depressions reach down to the moist rocks of an aquifer and water bubbles to the surface in cool pools, or where streams flow down from mountains to parched lowlands, vegetation grows and animals live.

Rivers and streams flowing away from rapidly eroding uplands can carry vast quantities of broken rock fragments in the form of grains of sand and silt. They are spread across the lowlands as the current slackens. The result may be accumulating beds of fertile soil in which plants grow. So, in desert areas, the river supports the riverside vegetation and the seasonal floods spread layers of silt over the landscape, fertilizing it. The River Nile, with its annual floods, keeps the Egyptian desert alive and was responsible for

producing one of the earliest prolific farming civilizations.

In Triassic times the vast supercontinent of Pangaea was beginning to break up. The interior was still arid, being so far from the sea, and life could only really flourish in the flood plains of rivers. It was the time of the prosauropods – the first big plant-eating dinosaurs – the early relatives of the huge long-necked sauropods. They fed on the cycad-like plants that grew close to the ground, and also reached up to browse the

coniferous trees that lined the water courses. This heavy browsing led to the evolution of trees and foliage that had strong, sharp, sword-like leaves as a defence, such as the monkey puzzle tree that still exists in the mountains of South America and in ornamental gardens across Europe. Among the predators, the various crocodile relatives, such as the phytosaurs, were giving way to the first of the theropods. When the plant-eaters were attracted to the water and became trapped in quicksands, their great weight preventing them from escaping, the meat-eaters would take advantage of their helplessness. Remains of all these animals are found in the rocks formed from the river sandstones and the silty flood deposits of the time. Occasionally their fossils tell the story of trapped animals devoured by predators, or even of animals killed by the changing seasonal conditions.

Below: A prosauropod, attracted to the water, is trapped in quicksand. Small theropods and crocodile-like predators close in for the kill.

Petrified Forest National Park

The most famous fossil occurrence of a Triassic desert waterside habitat is Petrified Forest National Park in Arizona, USA. Close by, at Ghost Ranch, a pack of meat-eating theropods, *Coelophysis*, was discovered as articulated skeletons. The evidence shows that they died from dehydration around a drying water hole. The best evidence for prosauropods being caught in quicksand and killed by predators comes from the Frick Brick Quarry, Switzerland. Almost identical circumstances are known from the Molento and Lower Elliot Formations of South Africa, showing how widespread these habitats were on Pangaea.

1 *Plateosaurus* – prosauropod dinosaur.
2 *Liliensternus* – theropod dinosaur.
3 *Rutiodon* – crocodile-like phytosaur.
4 Sauropod leg bones set vertically in river sandstones showing where they were caught in quicksands.
5 The rest of the skeleton torn apart and scattered.
6 Footprints of theropods.
7 Scattered teeth of theropods and phytosaurs.
8 Articulated skeletons of dinosaurs killed by drought.
9 Mud cracks revealing a drying water hole.
10 Burrows of worms and arthropods showing the presence of water.

CALM LAGOONS

Seawater trapped behind reefs forms shallow lagoons that evaporate slowly under a hot, tropical sun.
The salt concentration in the water increases and the water becomes toxic, killing anything that enters it.
Detailed evidence of life in dinosaur times comes from deposits formed under these conditions.

In late Jurassic times the break up of Pangaea was well under way. A huge embayment, known as the Tethys Sea, separated the continent of Europe and Asia from the landmasses of the south; those that became Africa, South America and Australia.

Along the northern flanks of the Tethys a deep-water reef developed, formed from sponges. The remains of this reef can be found today in rocks from Spain to Romania. As the reef grew, and as continental movements raised the sea floor, the reef approached the surface where the deep-water sponges died. The reef growth was continued by corals building on the sponge-formed

structures. The reefs reached the surface where they cut off lagoons between the deep Tethys waters and the shoreline at the continent to the north. Debris from the reefs filled the lagoons and the water became shallow. The heat of the sun evaporated the water from these shallows, and salt and other minerals settled on the lagoon floor. The water was constantly replenished from the ocean beyond the

Solnhöfen

There is a concentration of lagoon deposits in Solnhöfen, southern Germany. These so-called lithographic limestone quarries have yielded famous fossils of flying animals and land-living creatures. There are fossils of ammonites that have plunged into the limy mud, horseshoe crabs that have dropped dead at the end of their tracks, and floating animals, such as brittle stars and jellyfish, that drifted into the poisonous waters.

Right: This pterosaur fossil is from Solnhöfen, Germany. The details of its anatomy are clearly defined.

Below: The lagoon environment is best known from Solnhöfen, Germany, where some of the finest fossils have been uncovered, but lagoons of this kind probably extended across the whole of southern Europe.

reefs, but the lower layer of the lagoon water became poisonous with the concentration of minerals. Any fish that swam in it died and sank to the bottom. Any arthropod that crawled in was poisoned and died. The bodies lay undisturbed as the water was poisonous for scavengers too.

Islands were scattered across the lagoons which, with the arid shoreline, were formed from the stumps of the sponge reefs that had emerged from the water as the land rose. The animals of these dry lands consisted of pterosaurs, the first-known bird *Archaeopteryx*, little lizards and small dinosaurs, such as the chicken-sized theropod *Compsognathus*. All of these animals have been found as articulated skeletons in the deposits formed in the lagoons.

1 *Rhamphorhynchus* – rhamphorhynchoid pterosaur.
2 *Pterodactylus*.
3 *Archaeopteryx* – primitive bird.
4 *Compsognathus* – theropod dinosaur.
5 *Bavarisaurus* – lizard.
6 Articulated skeletons preserved in thinly-
    bedded limestone.

RIPARIAN FORESTS

Many dinosaur fossils from North America come from the late Jurassic Morrison Formation that stretches across much of the Midwest. It consists of river- and flood-deposits. Under seasonally dry conditions, vegetation was mostly restricted to river banks and only flourished in the wet season.

When the pioneers headed west across North America in the late nineteenth century, they found the bones of strange animals. The finds drew the attention of scientists who, within 30 years, discovered more than 100 previously unknown dinosaur types. Most came from a sequence of rocks called the Morrison Formation, which was formed from river sediments in late Jurassic times. The landscape was once that of a riparian forest. In the late Jurassic a shallow seaway stretched north-south along the length of the North American continent. To the west the ancestral Rocky

Mountains arose along the edge of the ocean. Between the two stretched a plain built up of sediment washed down from the mountains. Rivers meandered across the plain, flooding frequently and depositing sediment. In times of flood, the sediment built up on the riverbanks, forming levees, until the surface of the river became higher than the elevation of the surrounding plain. The water frequently broke through the levees spreading sediment in a fan-shaped deposit, and river water often seeped through the levees as springs filled freshwater ponds and lakes across the plain. Other lakes,

formed at times of flood, dried out and became poisonous with alkaline minerals leached from the soil.

Below: During the late Jurassic, in North America, in the wet seasons the rains were plentiful and floods spread across the plains. Flood sediment was deposited over the landscape causing prolific plant growth on which animals browsed.

The original flood deposits were disturbed by the trampling feet of the animals – called "bioturbation." The alkaline lakes formed beds of limestones with ribbons of river sediments running through them. Dinosaur fossils are found as isolated bones on the flood deposits or sometimes as associated skeletons in the river sediments.

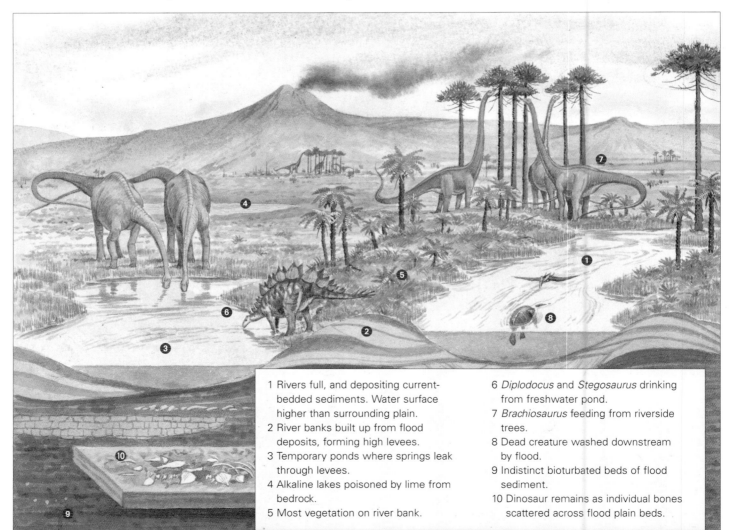

1 Rivers full, and depositing current-bedded sediments. Water surface higher than surrounding plain.
2 River banks built up from flood deposits, forming high levees.
3 Temporary ponds where springs leak through levees.
4 Alkaline lakes poisoned by lime from bedrock.
5 Most vegetation on river bank.
6 *Diplodocus* and *Stegosaurus* drinking from freshwater pond.
7 *Brachiosaurus* feeding from riverside trees.
8 Dead creature washed downstream by flood.
9 Indistinct bioturbated beds of flood sediment.
10 Dinosaur remains as individual bones scattered across flood plain beds.

Morrison Formation

The Morrison Formation, named after the Colorado town of Morrison, USA, consists of 30–275m (100–900ft) of shale, siltstone and sandstone, and stretches from Montana to New Mexico. Its landscape was once that of a riparian forest, or forest at the side of riverbanks. The most famous outcrops of the Morrison Formation are in Dinosaur National Monument in Utah, the Fruita Palaeontological Area and Dry Mesa Quarry, both in Colorado. At Tendaguru in Tanzania, a similar environment existed at exactly that time and almost the same range of animals lived there.

Above: The Morrison Formation is seen most obviously as a ridge along the foothills of the modern Rocky Mountains.

On this topographic surface the plants were confined largely to the river banks and around the freshwater pools. The plants formed forests and isolated stands of primitive conifers and ginkgos, with a lower-storey of cycad-like plants and tree ferns, and an undergrowth of ferns and beds of horsetails close to the water. The open plain had a scrappy growth of ferns. The alkaline pools were barren. The climate was seasonal with dry periods interrupted by times of abundant rain.

Herds of sauropods migrated across this landscape. *Diplodocus,* *Apatosaurus, Camarasaurus, Brachiosaurus* and many others, moved from thicket to thicket wherever there was food. The plated *Stegosaurus* fed from the trees and undergrowth. The main ornithopod was *Camptosaurus*. There were theropods aplenty, ranging from the enormous *Allosaurus*, through the medium-size *Ceratosaurus* to smaller animals like *Ornitholestes* and *Coelurus*. The abundant fossil remains of these dinosaurs are found mostly as isolated bones in flood deposits, but there are also associated skeletons and articulated skeletons in river channel deposits.

Below: In the dry season rivers dried to a trickle, and ponds became hard-packed mud. Water evaporation brought up the mineral calcite and left it as lumpy beds of limestone beneath the soil surface. Animals migrated into areas where there was still food to be had.

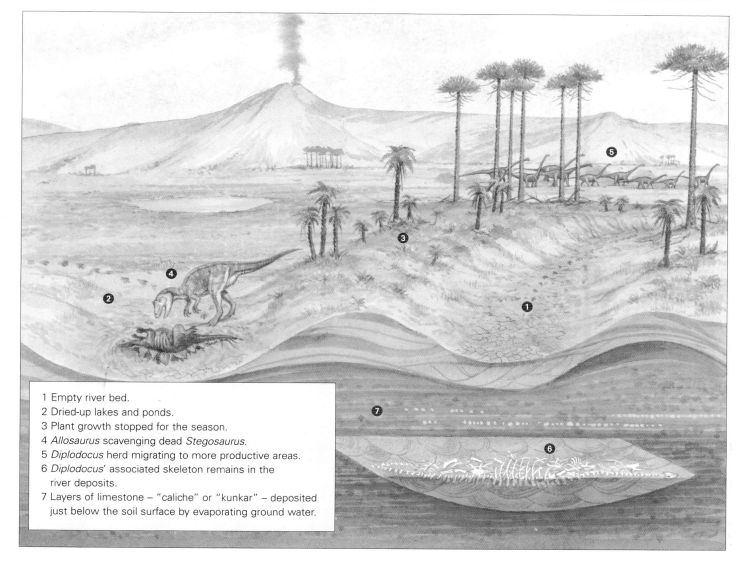

1 Empty river bed.
2 Dried-up lakes and ponds.
3 Plant growth stopped for the season.
4 *Allosaurus* scavenging dead *Stegosaurus*.
5 *Diplodocus* herd migrating to more productive areas.
6 *Diplodocus'* associated skeleton remains in the river deposits.
7 Layers of limestone – "caliche" or "kunkar" – deposited just below the soil surface by evaporating ground water.

LAKE ENVIRONMENTS

Lakes tend to be rather ephemeral. Water-filled hollows left by glaciers or landslide-blocked valleys soon fill with sediment and disappear. However, lakes formed in rift valleys, such as those in modern East Africa may be long-lasting landscape features. Good fossil remains are found in rift valley lake deposits.

At the end of the Jurassic period and the beginning of the Cretaceous, the eastern part of the northern continent, in the area where China now lies, was beginning to break up. The continental surface was split by fault lines, running north-east to south-west, which produced rift valleys. These rift valleys contained lakes. The water of these lakes was clear, and the only sediment was from very fine particles. In quiet times the valleys were filled with lush forests of long-needled conifers and ginkgoes. Horse-tails, ferns and mosses flourished around the lake edges. This environment supported an astonishing assortment of animals. The biggest were the dinosaurs, such as the

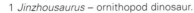

1 *Jinzhousaurus* – ornithopod dinosaur.
2 *Manchurochelys* – turtle.
3 *Eosipterus* – pterosaur.
4 *Beipiaosaurus* – therizinosaur dinosaur.
5 *Caudipteryx* – theropod dinosaur.
6 *Microraptor* – theropod dinosaur.
7 *Confuciusornis* – bird.
8 *"Fuzzy raptor"* – theropod dinosaur.
9 *Hyphalosaurus* – swimming lizard.
10 *Protosephurus* – fish.
11 Lakeside forests of conifers and ginkgoes.
12 Fine-grained beds of limestone.
13 Thicker beds of volcanic ash.
14 Animals perfectly preserved in beds of limestone beneath beds of ash.

horse-sized ornithopod *Jinzhousaurus*, which browsed the low plants of the shorelines. The hairy therizinosaur *Beipiaosaurus* hunted small animals on the banks. The smaller dinosaurs were theropods, many of which seemed to show transitional features between conventional dinosaurs and birds. *Sinosauropteryx* was like *Compsognathus* but covered in fur or feathers. *Caudipteryx* and

Below: Lake environments existed throughout the changing landscape of the Age of Dinosaurs. The lake deposits found in Liaoning, China, are beds of fine limestone interspersed with beds of volcanic ash that formed in early Cretaceous times.

Protarchaeopteryx had stubby wing-like forelimbs with feathers, and a fan of feathers on the tail. *Microraptor*'s fore and hind limbs even evolved into wings. There were also true birds, some of which still had primitive claws on the wings. These smaller creatures hunted the swarms of insects that lived close to the water.

We know of the existence of these animals because the mode of preservation is so fine that even the finest structures are visible. Every now and again the volcanoes that formed along the fault lines would erupt, engulfing the valleys in poisonous gas and showering the lakes with a thick deposit of ash. Gassed by volcanic

fumes and buried in fine volcanic ash, the smallest details of skin and feathers have been preserved around the almost perfectly articulated skeletons. We also have the fossils of their insect prey, and all sorts of other animals, such as turtles and other swimming reptiles, and also early mammals, that lived in the area.

WETLANDS

Wetlands tend to be most extensive in moist, tropical climates, close to upland areas. Heavy erosion from exposed hills brings masses of sediment down to low-lying regions. The sediment spreads out to form mud flats through which streams meander.

The most extensive, modern, tropical wetlands are found in the papyrus-choked Nile drainage area in Sudan and Uganda. Wetlands also appear further south in the Okovango flood plain at the edge of the Kalahari Desert. The mud flats support vegetation peculiarly adapted to the conditions. In these places the dominant plants are water-loving grasses and reeds, which developed in the Tertiary period. In the Mesozoic,

the water courses and mud banks supported thick beds of horsetails. Like grasses, horsetails spread by means of underground stems which held the sediments together, and provided a firm surface on which more permanent vegetation could grow. Like reeds, the horsetails could grow in shallow water. On stabilized sandbanks, thickets of ferns such as *Weichselia* grew. Stable ground developed and on it thrived thickets of conifers and cycads.

During the Cretaceous period, herds of *Iguanodon* roamed the wetlands of northern Europe, grazing on horsetail beds. Smaller herbivores, such as the fleet-footed *Hypsilophodon*, also scampered there. In the more permanent thickets, armoured dinosaurs such as *Polacanthus* grazed. Where plant-eating animals flourished,

Below: Dinosaur bones may be quite abundant and diverse in wetland deposits, but they tend to consist of isolated bones or, at best, associated skeletons.

European wetlands

The dinosaur wetlands of northern Europe are best represented by the Wealden and Wessex formations, laid down during the early Cretaceous. They outcrop along southern England and the Isle of Wight, and across the Paris Basin. At the time, mountains of limestone and metamorphic rock to the north supplied the sediment that washed down to the lowlands. The result is a thick sequence of sandstone, mudstone and clay, with frequent beds of plant-rich material. Dinosaur remains mostly occur as isolated bones, some showing signs of gnawing. They are often found with the teeth of freshwater fish, and are sometimes encrusted with the eggs of freshwater snails, showing that they were deposited in stream beds or in the backwaters of rivers.

meat-eaters that preyed on them followed, and in the horsetail swamps of northern Europe they included *Megalosaurus* and *Neovenator*. Wading in the waters were fish-eating theropods, such as *Baryonyx*.

Dinosaurs were not the only animals that existed here. In the water were crocodiles, including the dwarf form, *Bernissartia*, no bigger than a domestic cat, and turtles such as *Chitracephalus*, about the size of a dinner plate. In the skies there wheeled pterosaurs, such as the condor-sized *Ornithodesmus*. Disarticulated bones of all these animals have been found in the swamp deposits laid down at that time. The isolated fossil bones in these deposits may be worn and polished,

showing that they were washed about for a while before settling. They are sometimes encrusted with the eggs of water snails, suggesting that they lay on the stream bed for some time before becoming buried.

1 *Oviraptor* – theropod dinosaur.
2 *Eotyrannus* – theropod dinosaur.
3 *Neovenator* – theropod dinosaur.
4 *Bernissartia* – crocodile.
5 *Pelorosaurus* – sauropod dinosaur.
6 *Polacanthus* – armoured dinosaur.
7 *Baryonyx* – theropod dinosaur.
8 *Iguanodon* – ornithopod dinosaur.
9 *Hypsilophodon* – ornithopod dinosaur.
10 River and flood deposits.
11 Lens-shaped stream deposits.
12 Fossils appear as isolated bones in river deposits.

SWAMP FORESTS

By the end of the Cretaceous period the vegetation of the world was taking on an appearance familiar to humans. There were still no grasses, but flowering plants had appeared in the undergrowth, and deciduous trees were beginning to take over from conifers as the main woodland flora.

It is easy to imagine dinosaurs as being the inhabitants of deep, dark jungles. Where there were deep forests and woodlands, there were dinosaurs well adapted to living there. As the advanced ornithopods, especially the duckbills, evolved and diversified during the Cretaceous period, plant-life evolved with them. The broad mouths and low-slung necks of these ornithopods showed that they fed close to the ground. The evolutionary response would have been for plants, having been grazed, to develop survival strategies that would allow them to rebuild populations quickly. Flowers and enclosed seeds do this, allowing the main part of the germination process to take place after the parent has been destroyed. Flowering plants in deciduous woodlands evolved with the low-feeding habits of the later plant-eaters such as the broad-mouthed duckbills. Many of these dinosaurs had extravagant head structures, linked to their nasal passages. They made grunts and trumpet noises, producing sounds that would penetrate dense forest undergrowth so that the animals could communicate with one another.

The deciduous woodlands spread across the broad plains and deltas, between the newly arisen Rocky Mountains and the spreading inland sea, that now reached from the Arctic Ocean down across the middle of North America. The deposits formed the Hell Creek Formation. On higher ground the forests consisted of vegetation such as tall stands of primitive conifers with an understorey of cycads and ferns. These forests were inhabited by the last of the long-necked sauropods that had been the most important plant-eaters since the beginning of the Jurassic period.

Fossil survival

Duckbilled dinosaurs are sometimes found as 'mummies', with the skin still fossilized around them. This occurred when the animal died and was stranded in the open, possibly on a sandbank in a delta. One flank of the dead animal would be pressed down into the mud, impressing the skin texture into the mud. The insides would have shrivelled away and the skin would have dried to leather, shrinking around the bones of the leg and the rib cage. The exposed part of the skeleton would have deteriorated quickly, the bones carried off by scavengers or washed away in the river. The next flood would have filled its insides with sand swirled along by the floodwaters. Fish have been found fossilized inside the rib cages of such dinosaurs. The skin would not have survived the subsequent fossilization process but by then the impression in the surrounding sediment would have solidified. The result is an articulated skeleton that is surrounded by the impression of the skin, giving a valuable insight into what the outer covering of a dinosaur was like.

Below: All manner of creatures from the tiniest insects to the largest dinosaurs have been found fossilized in areas that were once river beds and swamps.

1 *Kritosaurus* – ornithopod dinosaur.
2 *Troodon* – theropod dinosaur.
3 *Tyrannosaurus* – theropod dinosaur.
4 *Ceramornis* – modern-type bird.
5 Skeleton of *Kritosaurus* drying out, with underside buried in mud.
6 Deciduous trees.
7 Flowering herbaceous undergrowth.
8 Swamp deposits.
9 Channel deposits.
10 Dinosaur remains appear as articulated or associated skeletons.

OPEN PLAINS

Herd-living animals have always lived on wide open plains. This was also true in dinosaur times. The late Cretaceous rocks formed on the plains of North America have ample evidence of herding behaviour in the horned dinosaurs – including the fossilization of entire herds in deposits known as "bonebeds".

Modern open landscapes are dominated by herds of plant-eating animals. Look at the high Serengeti plain of Tanzania today, with its herds of wildebeest, impala, elands, gazelles, zebras and so on. So it was with the open plains of the Cretaceous period.

The low vegetation that clothed the open landscapes in the Cretaceous period consisted largely of ferns but no grass. This was where herds of ceratopsians roamed. Like the modern herds that consist largely of different types of antelope, with different horn arrangements, the Cretaceous herds consisted of a number of different types of ceratopsian. They differed from one another by the arrangement of horns and frills, and other head ornamentation. The youngsters all looked the same – when they were young they were sheltered by the rest of the herd and had little contact with other ceratopsians. As adults, however, the range of horn and frill types was very marked. This suggests that the ceratopsians lived in tightly organized herds, moving from place to place as a unit, and keeping away from herds of other types, as happens in modern

grassland animals. Additionally, like the ceratopsians, modern grassland animals migrated with the seasons to where food was most abundant.

We can see evidence of herd behaviour in the fossil occurrences known as bonebeds. They consist of a mass of bones, usually of one species of ceratopsian. The bones lie on the bottom of stream channel deposits and tend to be of the same size, suggesting that they have been sorted out by flowing water. They may consist of the remains of more than 1,000 individuals of the same species. It is

Below: Herds of various species of ceratopsian roamed the plains of North America in the late Cretaceous, harassed by the big meat-eaters of the time.

easy to visualize the scenario. A herd of ceratopsians was overcome by water while crossing a river during migration, and the bodies were washed downstream. The bodies washed ashore on a river beach, where they decayed and were scavenged by other dinosaurs and pterosaurs. Then the remains were picked up by the flooding river and deposited on the channel bottom, along with shed teeth from the scavengers.

As modern plant-eaters have predators like lions to harass them, so the ceratopsians had the tyrannosaurs.

Dinosaur Provincial Park
The best-studied ceratopsian bone beds are in the late Cretaceous Dinosaur Park Formation, in Dinosaur Provincial Park, in Alberta, Canada, where there are at least eight occurrences, one stretching for almost 10km (6 miles). Others occur in Montana, USA, and as far north as the North Slope of Alaska.

Below: Dinosaur Provincial Park, Alberta.

1 *Chasmosaurus* in defensive circle.
2 *Albertosaurus*.
3 *Quetzalcoatlus* – pterosaur.
4 *Centrosaurus* in migrating herd.
5 *Styracosaurus* displaying to other ceratopsians.
6 Plain formed of flood sediments.
7 Lens-shaped channel deposits.
8 Bonebeds at the bases of channel deposits.

Formation of a bone bed
A Herd of ceratopsians crosses a river.
B Herd panics and individuals drown.
C Bodies are washed up on a sandbar.
D Bodies are scavenged by meat-eaters.
E Remains are washed into the river and settle on the bed.

SHORELINES AND ISLANDS

The edge of the sea is a popular habitat for modern birds. It was probably the same for their ancestors, the dinosaurs, though evidence is sparse. Shoreline deposits tend to be sparse and rather ephemeral since they are constantly disrupted by waves and tides.

In Cretaceous times the seaway that spread down the length of the North American continent stretched from Alaska to the Gulf of Mexico, splitting the dry land in two. In some areas the hinterland was thickly forested, and migrating dinosaurs travelled along the beaches where the walking was easier. North-south trackways have been found in Oklahoma, Colorado and New Mexico, USA. These discoveries have led to the concept of the "dinosaur freeway" – a beach migration route indicated by the consistent direction of Cretaceous dinosaur footprints. There are also others.

Island inhabitants

Crocodiles inhabited the rivers that opened out into the continental sea, and their toe marks have been found where they clawed their way across the river sediments. Birds found plenty to eat on the tidemarks, and their three-toed footprints abound. They can be distinguished from the footprints of small dinosaurs by their more splayed toes.

Out at sea, islands, as always, can support a variety of specialized life forms. Animals reach newly formed

Below: The sequence of early Cretaceous rocks known as the Dakota Group was formed as seashore deposits along the interior sea of contemporary North America. It is famous for its footprints and trackways.

Dinosaur Ridge

The most publicized exposure of the dinosaur freeway is Dinosaur Ridge, in the Rocky Mountain foothills, just a few kilometres west of Denver, Colorado.

islands by being rafted there on logs or other land debris. Also, an island that formed when an area of land was cut off by the sea usually retains some of the mainland's animal life. In either scenario, if the island becomes a permanent geographical feature the animal life will adapt and evolve to survive there. One such adaptation is the development of dwarf forms. Small animals need less food to survive, and islands have limited natural resources. In the Ice Age there were elephants the size of pigs on the Mediterranean islands, and giant ground sloths on the Caribbean islands that were much smaller than their mainland relatives. A modern example is the Shetland pony, a breed well adapted to the bleak habitat of the Scottish islands. The northern edge of the Tethys Sea in Europe had a whole archipelago of islands, thrown up by earth movements as the northern and southern continents approached one another. Bones of dinosaurs unearthed in Romania show that duckbills, only one-third of the size of their relatives, and ankylosaurs the size of sheep, existed there.

1 *Planicoxa* – ornithopod dinosaur.
2 *Acrocanthosaurus* – theropod dinosaur.
3 Pterodactyloid pterosaur.
4 Birds.
5 Alternating beds of beach sands and shallow sea sediments.
6 Sand ripples.
7 Ornithopod trackways following the shoreline as herds migrated.
8 Theropod trackways at right angles to the shoreline, as individuals came out of the forest to scavenge or to attack the migrating herds.
9 Bird trackways in random feeding pattern.
10 Individual dinosaur bones in sea sediments – badly worn and encrusted with sea life.

MOUNTAINS

Mountainous habitats in Mesozoic times would have had specific flora and fauna, adapted to high altitude environments with thin air, dryness and cold. Creatures from such habitats are rarely found as fossils, and so we can only speculate as to the animals and plants that lived in these regions at that time.

The Mesozoic world was continuously on the move. The shifting plates that tore Pangaea apart and made the continents drift crumpled up mountain ranges along the edge. The debris that formed the sediment of the sedimentary rocks of the time was worn from these Mesozoic mountains. These mountains would have had their share of animal life, as they do in the present day, and they must have had some dinosaurs.

What do we know of animals that lived in areas of erosion, rather than of deposition? What of animals that lived in mountains where no sediment was accumulating, and no rocks were being formed?

In modern times we can see how mountains produce particular habitats. Most rain falls on low ground, particularly on the windward sides of mountains. High up the rainfall becomes less and the temperatures drop. This affects the kinds of plants that grow and in turn the animal life. Mountain animals must be specifically adapted to the extremes of cold, and to clambering about on exposed rocks – the modern ibex is a good contemporary example. We expect that the dinosaurs living in the mountains would have been quite different from the well-known ones that lived in the lowlands, but there has been speculation.

We know the bonehead dinosaurs by the fossil skulls that have been found. This is unusual – the skulls of dinosaurs are usually the first to break down and disappear when the animal fossilizes. The boneheads had skulls thick enough to withstand all sorts of taphonomic punishment. Many of them are found badly worn, as if they had been rolled along river beds for a long time before coming to rest and being buried. It is possible that the home ranges of the boneheads were well inland, and perhaps in mountainous areas where the streams had their sources.

Ankylosaur skeletons are often found lying on their backs in marine sediments. It seems likely that their dead bodies had been drifting down rivers for a long time – long enough for decay to begin. When the gases of putrefaction expanded in the body

cavity the floating animal would have rolled on its back, the armour acting as a keel. Eventually it would have sunk to the bottom in this attitude. Again it is possible that the dead animals were carried downstream from mountainous areas where they lived. All this, however, is mere speculation. It is one of the reasons why we will only find the remains of a fraction of the dinosaurs that ever lived.

Below: Mountains are areas of erosion rather than of deposition, and so no sedimentary rocks would have accumulated there, and hence no fossils would have been preserved. Herds of boneheads and solitary ankylosaurs may have roamed the slopes, while pterosaurs would have soared overhead.

1 Mountain conifer.
2 Meadow of heath-like or moor-like vegetation.
3 *Quetzalcoatlus* – pterosaur.
4 *Stegoceras* – bonehead dinosaur.
5 *Edmontonia* – ankylosaur dinosaur.
6 Scree slope – rubble formed as erosive forces break down the mountain rocks and carry them away.

EXTINCTION

What happened 65 million years ago, at the end of the Cretaceous period has always been a mystery.
After 155 million years as the most prominent animal life on Earth, the dinosaurs suddenly died out.
With them, flying and swimming reptiles, a large number of fish and other animals disappeared.

There have been many theories regarding the reasons behind the extinction of the dinosaurs. Mostly the theorists have been divided into two camps – those who favour gradual extinction as an explanation and those who favour sudden catastrophe, although "sudden", in geological terms, can actually cover half a million years, looking instantaneous in the geological record.

The gradualists stress that for most of the late Cretaceous period, conditions had been very stable, with not much variation in climate for tens of millions of years. It may be that the specialized animal life of the time had become too specialized and too adapted to these stable conditions. A slight change in the environment, such as the raising of the temperature or the cooling of the atmosphere, may have put intolerable stresses on the dinosaurs so that they could not cope.

The corresponding change of vegetation that would have accompanied a climatic change would have resulted in a change in dinosaur food stocks and as a result the dinosaurs could have starved.

Above: One theory suggests that climatic conditions changed at the end of the Cretaceous, killing the dinosaurs.

Another theory suggests that the gradual movement of continents brought landmasses into close proximity to one another. As a result animals would have been able to migrate and carry with them, into new geographical regions, diseases to which the endemic population would have been vulnerable.

Below and left: Another theory backed by scientific understanding is that a meteor hit the Earth's surface, resulting in huge changes to the Earth's atmosphere and the extinction of the dinosaurs. The meteor is said to have caused the Chicxulub Crater, at the edge of the Gulf of Mexico.

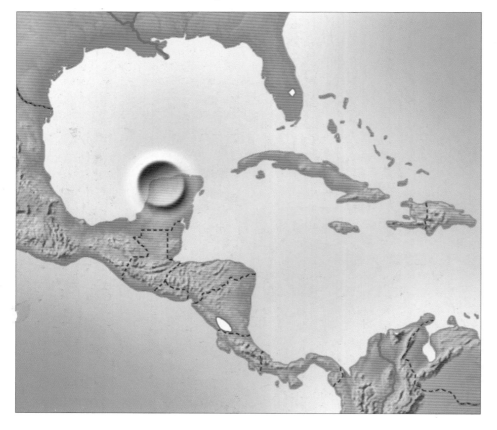

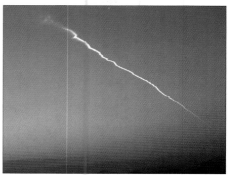

Above: A third theory suggests that volcanic activity caused the death of the dinosaurs.

Above: The eruptions that caused vast lava flows in Creaceous India would have altered the climate considerably.

However, some view the demise of the dinosaurs as a sudden occurrence. They envisioned cataclysms brought about by violent volcanic eruptions, or earthquakes producing such extreme conditions that the dinosaurs could not have coped. However, then, in the 1970s, a discovery was made that changed this discussion for ever. It was found that the end of the Cretaceous and the beginning of the Tertiary (the K/T boundary in geological parlance) was marked by a bed that was rich in the element iridium. Iridium is rare at the surface of the Earth but quite common in meteorites. So a new theory was put forward that a massive meteorite had struck the Earth 65 million years ago. The immediate result would have been shock waves and fires. The explosion would have sent masses of dust and steam into the atmosphere, blanketing the Earth and causing temperatures to fall as the sunlight was blocked out. Plants would have died. Plant-eating dinosaurs would have starved. Then meat-eating dinosaurs, denied their plant-eating prey, would have perished. After months or years the skies would have cleared and plants would have started to grow. By that time all the dinosaurs would be dead.

A huge buried structure, on the coast of Yucatan in Mexico, was identified as a meteorite crater dating from the end of the Cretaceous period. Signs of shattered rocks and sea wave damage were identified around the Caribbean. Corroborative evidence was being amassed.

Other theories were put forward too. Iridium is also found beneath the Earth's crust, and could be brought out by volcanic activity. There was indeed a great deal of volcanic activity at that time – half of the continent of India is made up of lava flows that erupted just then. Volcanic activity as intense as that could have had exactly the same effect as a meteorite strike, blanketing the Earth with smoke and fumes. India and Yucatan were on exactly opposite sides of the globe 65 million years ago. A massive meteorite impact in one could have sent shock waves through the crust and instigated volcanic activity in the other. Or the meteorite could have split into two, one part falling in India, the other in Yucatan. In any case, the theories of those who believe in catastrophe are popular.

However, there were other subtleties. Statistical analysis of fossil finds suggested that the dinosaurs had been dying out for several million years before the end of the Cretaceous.

Perhaps they were already on their way out when an impact just finished them off. Whatever the cause, the reign of the dinosaurs came to an end. The land was swept clear, to be colonized by something else. The something else turned out to be the mammals – small, insignificant creatures while the dinosaurs were alive, but adaptable enough to take over once they had gone. As a result they evolved and spread and took over every niche that had been previously occupied by the dinosaurs.

Below: Volcanic eruptions occurred throughout the Age of Dinosaurs, for example, producing the Triassic ash beds seen here. However, none was so great as that which occurred at the end.

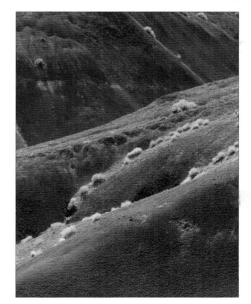

THE FOSSILIZATION PROCESS

After an animal dies and its body is subjected to the different destructive forces of taphonomy, what is left may be fossilized. This process involves the burial and preservation of the remains. The sediments in which the remains are buried become sedimentary rock, and the original remains are turned into mineral.

Taphonomy is the study of what happens to an organism after its recent death and before it becomes a fossil. Diagenesis is what happens thereafter to turn what remains of the body into something that will withstand the passage of time.

The fossils that we pick up from the rocks, or that we see in museums, have changed a great deal in substance and appearance since they were parts of living organisms.

Fossil formation

The fossil is formed at the same time as the sediment in which the organism lies is turned to sedimentary rock. This diagenesis usually involves two processes – compression and cementation. Compression is produced by the sheer weight of the overlying sediments, and acts to compact the grains of the sediment into a more coherent mass. In cementation, the ground water percolating through the rock deposits mineral, often calcite (the same as builders' cement), between the grains gluing them together as a solid mass. Further compaction and the input of heat from the Earth's interior may alter the mineral content of the rock. If this

happens it will take the rock from the realms of a sedimentary rock to a metamorphic rock, a new type in which usually all the fossils are destroyed.

In the rare occurrences in which an embedded organism becomes a fossil in a sedimentary rock, one of a number of different processes may be involved. An organism, or part of an organism, may remain unaltered. This is a very rare form of fossilization, but we sometimes see it in an insect preserved in a piece of amber. The procedure is simple. An insect settles on a glob of resin seeping from a tree and becomes trapped. It is engulfed and preserved before it has a chance to decay. Later the resin becomes buried and turned into amber through the normal processes that turn sediment to rock, and the insect is preserved within. Sometimes, though, this perfect preservation is illusory for the insects innards may have decayed through the action of its own bacteria. There are no dinosaur fossils that have been

preserved like this, and no dinosaur blood in preserved mosquito stomachs.

The hard parts of an organism may, however, remain unaltered. We find this in the teeth of sharks from the last few tens of millions of years. The teeth are so much tougher than the rest of the skeleton that they survive for a long period. The bones of Ice Age mammals trapped in the tar pools of Los Angeles are another example. Again, no dinosaurs are preserved like this. Sometimes only the original carbon of the organic substance remains. This is seen in the black shapes of leaves that are sometimes seen in plant fossils. Taken to an extreme, this process gives us coal.

Below: Over subsequent years mud and sand are deposited by flooding. The movement of the sediment means that the skeleton begins to break up and be dispersed. The skeleton is still white, fresh bone.

Below: In a dry season the following year, the vegetation has not survived, the river has dried up and mud cracks appear in the mudbanks, and the dinosaur's body is now a skeleton. The neck and tail are pulled back, as the tendons have dried and shrunk. Other scavenging dinosaurs take the last bits of nutrition from the skeleton.

Below: A dinosaur's body is washed up on a river sandbank. It has been dead a few days, and its stomach is bloated by decomposition. Beneath its body are the river sands.

Over long periods of time, the cellular structure of the original may be replaced by a totally different substance. Silica in ground-water passing through rocks may replace the original carbon, molecule by molecule, and give a fossil that shows the

Below: Eventually the skeleton is buried so deep below the surface that the sediments become rock and the skeleton becomes a fossil. The previously white skeleton turns black as the bone becomes mineralized. Above the dinosaur may be river sands and muds, beds of conglomerate (fossilized shingle), and marine limestone.

original microscopic structure, but made of silica. Petrified wood is a good example. It is also seen in some Australian plesiosaurs, in which the bone has been replaced by opal.

Groundwater percolating through the rock may also dissolve away all traces of the original organism. The result is a hole in the rock called a "mould", in exactly the same shape as the original. Permian reptiles from the desert sandstones of Elgin, in Scotland,

Below: The mountain is rising. The sedimentary rocks are uplifted and distorted. The skeleton is distorted too.

occur in this way, and pouring latex into the moulds produces casts of the original bones. This casting is sometimes done naturally, with dissolved groundwater minerals filling the moulds. Sea urchins in chalk are sometimes found replaced by flint. Then there are fossils which contain no part or impression of the original animal at all. They are called trace fossils and encompass footprints and trackways, coprolites and eggs.

All these processes mean nothing to us unless the fossil is returned to the surface. This only happens when the rocks containing the fossil are uplifted through earth movements, usually mountain building associated with the movement of the tectonic plates. Then erosion has to wear away all the rocks above so that the fossil is exposed. If this erosion is too vigorous, the exposed fossil will not last for long as it will be eroded away as well. All in all, even if a dinosaur does become fossilized, the odds are very much against our finding and excavating it. There are good reasons why dinosaur fossils are rare.

Below: Tens of millions of years later the rocks erode, revealing the fossilized skeleton.

EXCAVATION IN THE FIELD

Once the fossil dinosaur is discovered, the job of excavation can take on military-style logistics. Not only does the skeleton have to be extracted without damage, but the setting and the surrounding rocks must be analysed as well to give as full a picture as possible.

Usually a dinosaur skeleton is found by chance, by somebody out walking, or by a quarry worker turning over a rock. A *Stegosaurus* in Colorado was found recently when a palaeontologist working on another dig threw his hammer at random into a cliff. Another, in Montana, was found by a farmer digging a hole for a fence post. Once found, the skeleton is reported to a museum, a university or another institution that has the means to excavate it. Planning can take months or even years, and much of this involves finding the money to do the work – because practical palaeontology can be a very expensive business.

On site, the first thing is to find out how much of the skeleton there is. The overburden – that is the rock directly over the skeleton – has to be removed. This can be done with earth movers. Then, when the rock is down to a few centimetres of the bed that contains

Below: A palaeontologist marks out a grid over the bones, providing a reference to all finds in preparation for drawing a site map.

Above: Bones, jacketed in plaster, await their transportation to the laboratory.

the skeleton, the last of the overburden is removed carefully by hand, usually with fine tools and brushes.

Once the skeleton has been exposed, the next phase is to catalogue what is there. A site map is drawn. This is a plan of the site showing where each

bone lies, and the presence of anything else that may be of interest. Only when all this has been done can the excavation begin. Fossils that are newly exposed to the air may be very fragile. They may be unstable, and chemicals in them may react with the atmosphere and cause the fossil to decay quickly. Exposed bones are treated as quickly as possible with a chemical or varnish to seal them, and stop the air causing deterioration. The exact nature of the chemical or varnish has to be recorded for the technicians at the laboratory or the museum.

Fossil bones can be so fragile that they crumble away if they are lifted. To avoid this, they are encased in a jacket. It consists of a layer of moist paper, then a layer of plaster bandages – just like the plaster cast used in medicine for repairing a broken limb. (In the days of the "bone wars", this technique was pioneered by a fossil hunter, using rice, the staple food of

the expedition.) The exposed part of the bone is covered in this plaster jacket. Then the rock surrounding and underlying it is dug away, the bone turned over, and the rest of the jacket applied to the other side. How many jackets, and how big a part is jacketed at one time, will depend on the state of the skeleton. In an associated skeleton nearly every individual bone needs to be jacketed. If the skeleton is articulated and there is access to heavy lifting equipment, the whole skeleton can be jacketed in one go. The complete Colorado *Stegosaurus* mentioned above was airlifted from the site by helicopter, but it is rare for such expensive resources to be put at the disposal of a dinosaur excavation.

Once the skeleton has been removed the adjacent area is sifted for other specimens. Palaeontologists will look for the teeth of animals that may have scavenged the skeleton, the seeds of the plants that lived at the same time, and all sorts of other information that can be used to build up a picture of the animal's life.

Back in the laboratory, preparators, the technicians skilled in handling fossil material, prepare the fossil so

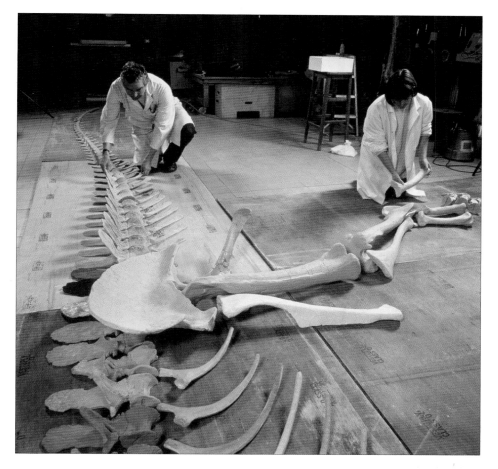

Below: The mounted skeleton of Triceratops is exhibited in life-like pose. It is made from a cast of the fossils.

Above: A mounted skeleton of Baryonyx is being prepared for exhibition. The casts, made of glass-reinforced plastic, are a lightweight material better suited to exhibition.

that it can be studied by the palaeontologist. Jackets are removed from the skeleton, and any stabilizing chemical is removed or replaced with one that is more appropriate for laboratory study.

In the past, the ultimate result was a mounted skeleton, with the fossil bones clamped to a welded steel frame erected in the public display area of a museum. Today a display skeleton is formed using casts of the skeleton rather than the actual fossils. Technicians make moulds from the fossils and cast reproductions of the bones in a lightweight material that is easier to handle, and which can be mounted more efficiently. This allows for the fossils to be stored under controlled conditions and kept available for study. Missing bones are replaced by casts from other skeletons, or sculpted by artists.

THE PALAEONTOLOGISTS

There are many hundreds of palaeontologists, the scientists who have discovered and studied the fossils, who should receive a mention in this list, all having pushed forward the frontiers of the science or still actively doing so. The following is merely a selection of those who have contributed to the science.

Florentino Ameghino
(1857–1911)

More famous for his work on the unique fossil mammals of South America, Ameghino pioneered the study and excavation of dinosaurs and other extinct vertebrates in Argentina in the late nineteenth century. Most of his discoveries are now housed in the La Plata Museum, Argentina.

Roy Chapman Andrews
(1884–1960)

Andrews led several expeditions from the American Museum of Natural History into the Gobi desert in the 1920s. The intention was to find the earliest remains of human ancestors. Instead he found a vast array of new dinosaurs in Cretaceous rocks. Perhaps the most important find was the first example of a dinosaur nest with its eggs. He pioneered the use of motorized transport to reach fossil sites.

Robert T. Bakker (1945–)

The concept of warm-bloodedness in dinosaurs is associated more with the charismatic Bakker than anyone else. Since the 1960s he has maintained that dinosaurs were lively active animals, using many lines of evidence, including comparative anatomy and fossil population studies. He has named several new dinosaur genera.

Rinchen Barsbold (1935–)

Barsbold is a Mongolian palaeontologist who, since the 1980s has worked with the Palaeontological Centre, Mongolian Academy

Camarasaurus *discovered by Cope.*

of Sciences, Ulan Baatar, and has done a great deal to uncover and name the central Asian dinosaurs.

José F. Bonaparte (1928–)

The most famous contemporary Argentinean palaeontologist, Bonaparte has added hugely to the understanding of dinosaurs in South America. His work includes studies of the late Cretaceous armoured titanosaurs and an investigation of South American pterosaurs that led to a renaissance of the subject.

William Buckland (1784–1856)

The first professor of geology at Oxford University, Buckland was the first to publish a scientific description of a dinosaur – *Megalosaurus* in 1824. Dinosaur bones had been noted before but never studied seriously. He recognized that the fossil jawbone and teeth that had been brought to him had come from a giant reptile of some kind. This was before the concept of a dinosaur had been established.

Edwin Colbert (1905–2001)

This curator of the American Museum of Natural History and later the Museum of Northern Arizona is famous for his discovery, in the 1960s, of the fossil of a mammal-like reptile, *Lystrosaurus*, in Antarctica. This discovery helped to confirm the

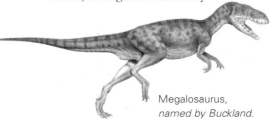

Megalosaurus, *named by Buckland.*

understanding of the movements of the continents caused by plate tectonics. He famously studied the bonebed of *Coelophysis* found in New Mexico.

Edward Drinker Cope (1840–97)

Cope was one of the two figures in the nineteenth century "bone wars" – a long-lasting rivalry with Othniel Charles Marsh to find and describe as many dinosaur specimens from the newly-opened Midwest of North America as possible. He worked from Philadelphia, USA.

Earl Douglass (1862–1931)

Douglass worked for the Carnegie Museum, in Pittsburgh, USA, (set up by the Scottish industrialist and philanthropist Andrew Carnegie to accommodate the dinosaur remains discovered in the Midwest at the end of the nineteenth century) and opened up the dinosaur beds of Utah. The site that he studied eventually became Dinosaur National Monument.

Eberhard Fraas (1862–1915)

Most dinosaur discoveries had been made in Europe and in North America. Fraas, a German authority on dinosaurs sent an expedition, led by Werner Janensch, to German East Africa (now Tanzania) in 1907 and uncovered the Jurassic dinosaur deposits at Tendaguru, including the huge *Brachiosaurus* (now renamed *Giraffatitan*) that for years stood in the Humboldt Museum in Berlin as the biggest mounted skeleton in the world.

John R. (Jack) Horner (1946–)

As state geologist for Montana, USA, Horner was the principal investigator of the dinosaur nesting sites of Egg Mountain and Egg Island, and named *Maiasaura*. The result of his work has been a new understanding of dinosaur family and social life.

Joseph Leidy (1823–91)

The first dinosaur to be studied in North America, was found in New Jersey, and named by Leidy. *Hadrosaurus* is now regarded as a *nomen dubium* as there was no skull to identify it. Leidy was based in Philadelphia and went on to name more dinosaurs. He is best known for his work on fossil Tertiary mammals.

Gideon Mantell (1790–1856)

As a country doctor in south-east England, Mantell collected fossils in his spare time. He and his wife Mary Ann found the bones of *Iguanodon* and named it in 1825. As time went on he spent less time as a doctor and devoted his time to amassing fossil collections, which he established in Brighton.

Othniel Charles Marsh (1831–99)

Marsh was Cope's opponent in the "bone wars", working from Yale University. They sent rival teams to sites to try to outdo one another. Before this time there had been only six genera of dinosaurs described. By the time the frenzy of the bone wars was over there were more than 130.

Herman von Meyer (1801–1896)

The first German palaeontologist, von Meyer described and named the first bird *Archaeopteryx*, as well as some of the

Maiasaura was named by John R Horner.

pterosaurs from the same area of southern Germany. He also discovered *Plateosaurus*, and pioneered the study of dinosaurs as well as invertebrate fossils in Germany and northern Europe.

John H. Ostrom (1928–2005)

With his discovery and description of *Deinonychus* in 1969, American palaeontologist Ostrom established the evolutionary connection between birds and dinosaurs. This also gave rise to the theory that the dinosaurs, at least the theropods, were warm-blooded like birds. The theory was eventually vindicated by the discoveries of the feathered dinosaurs and dinosaur-like birds in China.

Richard Owen (1804–92)

It was Sir Richard Owen, a British anatomist working at the British Museum (Natural History) – now the Natural History Museum – who is credited with creating the concept of dinosaurs by announcing at a meeting of the British Association for the Advancement of Science, in 1841, a new group of animals named the Dinosauria – based on *Megalosaurus*, *Iguanodon* and the ankylosaur *Hylaeosaurus*, which was also found by Mantell.

Ernst Stromer von Reichenbach (1870–1952)

This German palaeontologist from Munich was the first to excavate the dinosaur sites of Egypt. He did so for 30 years discovering such dinosaurs as *Aegyptosaurus*, *Carcharodontosaurus* and *Spinosaurus*. His specimens were lost during World War II when the museum in Munich was bombed. His excavation sites were forgotten too, until rediscovered by a team from Washington University in 2000.

Anserimimus discovered by Barsbold.

Harry Govier Seeley (1839–1909)

A British palaeontologist, his main contribution to palaeontology was to divide the dinosaurs into the orders Saurischia and Ornithischia based on their hip structures. He named a number of dinosaurs, but most were so fragmentary that they have been renamed or declared *nomen dubia*. He also published an early pioneering account of pterosaurs.

Paul Sereno (1957–)

Perhaps the most prolific dinosaur hunter today, Sereno, based in Chicago, USA, has discovered new dinosaurs in North Africa and in central Asia. In 1986 he advanced the understanding of dinosaurs by reclassifying the ornithischians in a system that is still used today.

Charles H. Sternberg (1850–1943) and his sons, Charles M., George and Levi

Charles senior contributed to the bone wars by excavating for Cope. Between 1912 and 1917, the family pioneered the Canadian boom in dinosaur discoveries. The skeletons that they extracted are displayed in museums all around the world.

Dong Zhiming (1937–)

The most famous modern Chinese palaeontologist, Dong opened up the vast dinosaur beds of Sichuan and in north-west China. Working with the Institute of Vertebrate Palaeontology and Palaeoanthropology in Beijing, China, he named about 20 new dinosaur genera in as many years. Among his wealth of discoveries he established the homalocephalid family of boneheaded dinosaurs.

Coelphysis, named by Cope but extensively studied by Colbert.

1 *Iguanodon*.
2 *Istiodactylus*
3 *Hypsolophodon*.
4 *Neovenator*.
5 *Bernissartia*.
6 *Eotyrannus*.

THE WORLD OF DINOSAURS

For 155 million years dinosaurs evolved and became one of the most successful groups of animals the world has ever known. They changed as the world around them changed.

At the beginning of the Age of Dinosaurs, during the late Triassic period, all the land areas of the Earth were fused together as a single landmass that we term the supercontinent of Pangaea. The centre of this supercontinent was searing desert, and the only habitable zones were around the edges. It is against this background that the dinosaurs developed. Since there was only one landmass, the same dinosaurs lived in all of the habitable areas – the prosauropods whose skeletons we find in Triassic Germany are largely the same as those we find in South Africa; the small theropods that existed in Arizona are almost identical to those in Zimbabwe.

Then, with the beginning of the Jurassic, the supercontinent began to split, opening up rift valleys that let the ocean into the heart of the landmass. Shallow seas spread over the margins giving broad continental shelves. The climate became moist. New types of dinosaur evolved in these conditions.

Finally, in the Cretaceous period, Pangaea had split into individual continents, most of which we would recognize today. As a result, different dinosaurs evolved in different areas, with the giant theropods of North America being of quite different families from the giant theropods of South America, and the long-necked sauropods of the southern continents being replaced by the duckbills as the main plant-eaters in the north. The biodiversity of the world was much greater at the end of the Age of Dinosaurs than it was at the beginning.

Against this changing background we can apply all the lines of evidence we have seen in the introductory chapters and study the dinosaurs that lived in different places at different times. The directory that follows depicts a selection of the dinosaurs known. However, new dinosaurs are being found all the time, and a catalogue such as this will require constant updating. There are many, many more dinosaurs that are still to be found.

Left: Early Cretaceous Europe had herds of large and small plant-eaters, menaced by large and small meat-eaters, along with their relatives, the crocodiles and the pterosaurs.

EARLY MEAT-EATERS

The theropods were the meat-eating dinosaurs, and existed throughout the Mesozoic. They first appeared in late Triassic times as smallish animals – about the size of foxes and wolves. In the subsequent Jurassic many of them became large, feeding on the big plant-eaters of the time. Then in the early Cretaceous they diversified, evolving into all kinds of different forms to exploit different food sources.

Eoraptor

The Valley of the Moon in north-western Argentina consists of dusty outcrops of sandstone and mudstone laid down in lushly forested river valleys in late Triassic times. These river banks were prowled by the first dinosaurs, including fox-sized *Eoraptor*, and various other reptiles that it hunted for food.

Right: Even the most perfect dinosaur skeleton can say little about the skin or the coloration. As in most restorations, skin colour and pattern are conjectural.

Features: *Eoraptor* is known from a complete skeleton that is lacking only the tail, and in shape and size *Eoraptor* conforms to every idea of the primitive dinosaur. Its lower jaw lacks the bone joint behind the tooth row that is seen in every other meat-eater, and there is more than one kind of tooth, something unusual in a meat-eating dinosaur. However, all other skeletal features such as the shape of the hips, the upright stance and a reduction of the number of fingers on the hand show that this dinosaur is definitely an early theropod.

Distribution: North-western Argentina.
Classification: Saurischia, Theropoda.
Meaning of name: Dawn plunderer.
Named by: Sereno, 1993.
Time: Carnian stage of the late Triassic.
Size: 1m (3ft).
Lifestyle: Hunter.
Species: *E. lunensis*.

Herrerasaurus

Distribution: North-western Argentina.
Classification: Saurischia, Theropoda, Herrerasauridae.
Meaning of name: From Victorio Herrera, its discoverer.
Named by: Sereno, 1988.
Time: Carnian stage of the late Triassic.
Size: 5m (16½ft).
Lifestyle: Hunter.
Species: *H. ischigualestensis*.

A contemporary of *Eoraptor* on the late Triassic riverbanks of Argentina, *Herrerasaurus* was a much bigger and more advanced theropod. Because of the difference in size, it must have hunted different prey from its smaller relative. Its skeleton was found in 1959, although it was several decades before it was scientifically studied. The complete skull was not found until 1988.

Features: A big animal with heavy jaws and 5cm- (2in-) long serrated teeth, giving it the appearance and probable lifestyle of the big theropods to come. It has the hinged lower jaw of other theropods. The foot bones are quite primitive, retaining the first and fifth toes that later theropods were to lose. *Herrerasaurus* has complex ear bones suggesting that it had a keen sense of hearing which would help in hunting.

Allosaurus

The most well-known of the late Jurassic theropods must be *Allosaurus*. It was unearthed by Othniel Charles Marsh during the "bone wars", and since then many specimens have been found. The Cleveland-Lloyd quarry alone has yielded more than 44 individuals. Species attributed to *Allosaurus* have been found as far away as Tanzania and Portugal. Sauropod bones have been found bearing marks gouged by *Allosaurus* teeth.

Features: *Allosaurus* is a familiar animal, with massive hind legs, strong S-shaped neck, a huge head with jaws that could bulge sideways to bolt down great chunks of meat; sharp, serrated, steak-knife teeth with 5cm- (2in-) long crowns; and short, heavy arms with three-fingered hands

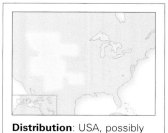

Distribution: USA, possibly Portugal and Tanzania.
Classification: Theropoda, Tetanurae, Carnosauria.
Meaning of name: Different lizard.
Named by: Marsh, 1877.
Time: Tithonian to Kimmeridgian stages of the late Jurassic.
Size: 12m (39ft).
Lifestyle: Hunter or scavenger.
Species: *A. tendagurensis, A. fragilis, A. amplexus, A. trihedrodon, A. whitei* and *A. (Saurophaganax) maximus*?

bearing ripping claws that were up to 15cm (6in) long. This enormous carnivore would have hunted the biggest plant-eaters of the time including the massive sauropods, the remains of which were found in the Cleveland-Lloyd quarry.

Right: Allosaurus *fossils have been found at sites in Colorado, Montana, New Mexico, Oklahoma, South Dakota, Utah and Wyoming, USA.*

CLEVELAND-LLOYD QUARRY

The Cleveland-Lloyd quarry lies 38km (30 miles) south of Price, Utah, close to the community of Cleveland. Dinosaur excavations started on the site in 1929 and over the next 10 or 12 years they continued thanks to financing by Malcolm Lloyd, a Philadelphia lawyer.

The University of Utah began a thorough excavation in 1960, headed by William Lee Stokes, and another in 2001 with Utah state geologist James H. Madsen in charge. The site was designated a National Natural Landmark in 1966. The excavations are open to view by the public, and skeletons from the site are on view in more than 60 museums worldwide.

The skeletons found at the site include sauropods and stegosaurs, but most appear to be the bones of meat-eaters. It is possible that the site represents a watering hole in an abandoned river meander on an arid Jurassic plain. Such a site would have attracted plant-eating animals from all over, and the meat-eaters would have converged, finding easy pickings among the weak and dehydrated sauropods and stegosaurs. The mud of the water hole would have hampered any escape. The skeletons appear to have been torn apart on the spot, and the bones show signs of having been trampled underfoot. Subsequent floods would have buried all this and set the fossilization process in motion.

Saurophaganax

The few bones known of *Saurophaganax* were excavated in the 1930s, but were not studied seriously until the 1990s. It turned out to be very similar to *Allosaurus* but a great deal bigger. After Don Chure's naming of it in 1995, David K. Smith re-analysed it in 1998 and came to the conclusion that it represented a particularly big species of *Allosaurus*.

Features: The description of *Allosaurus* can just as well apply to *Saurophaganax*, so close are the two animals. The differences lie in the sheer size of *Saurophaganax*, and in the shape of the neck and tail vertebrae. A complete mounted skeleton of *Saurophaganax* is on display in the Sam Noble Museum, in Oklahoma City, but most of it is made up of sculpted bones scaled up from those of the *Allosaurus* from the Cleveland-Lloyd quarry.

Distribution: Oklahoma, USA.
Classification: Theropoda, Tetanurae, Carnosauria.
Meaning of name: The greatest reptile-eater.
Named by: Chure, 1995.
Time: Kimmeridgian stage of the late Jurassic.
Size: 12m (39ft).
Lifestyle: Hunter or scavenger.
Species: *S. maximus*.

Spinosaurus

The first remains of this remarkable animal were found in Egypt by a German expedition in 1911, and were then lost when the Alte Akademie museum in Munich, Germany, in which it was stored, was destroyed by bombing in 1944. In 1996 Canadian palaeontologist Dale Russell found more remains in Morocco. As the villain of the film *Jurassic Park III*, *Spinosaurus* caught the public's imagination in 2001.

Right:
In early books
Spinosaurus *is restored with a short deep head, like that of a carnosaur. That was before the discovery of skull material in Morocco, and the realization of how closely related* Spinosaurus *was to the others of the group whose skulls were well known.*

Features: The most significant feature of the skeleton of *Spinosaurus* is the array of spines sticking up from the backbone, reaching heights of almost 2m (6½ft). In life this would have been covered by skin to form a fin or a sail. It may have acted as a heat regulation device, absorbing warmth from the sun or shedding excess body heat into the wind. It may also have been brightly coloured and used for signalling.

Distribution: Egypt and Morocco.
Classification: Theropoda, Spinosauridae.
Meaning of name: Spined lizard.
Named by: Stromer, 1915.
Time: Albian to Cenomanian stages of the Cretaceous.
Size: Maybe up to 17m (56ft).
Lifestyle: Fish hunter, predator or scavenger.
Species: *S. aegyptiacus*, *S. maroccansus*.

SPINOSAURID JAWS

The jaws and teeth of the spinosaurids are very different from those of any other meat-eating dinosaur. The snout is extremely narrow and very long. The teeth are much straighter than those of other meat-eaters, and on the lower jaw

Top: Inside jaw view.
Above: The spinosaurid upper jaw with teeth.

they are very numerous and small. The tip of the upper jaw carries a separate rosette of teeth that corresponds with a hooked structure at the tip of the lower jaw. The nostrils are placed well back on the snout.

These adaptations seem to have been well suited for catching fish. The narrow snout would cleave the water, the small sharp teeth would seize small, slippery prey, and the nostrils would be clear of the surface. In the modern world we see adaptations such as these in the gavial of the Far East. They are also present in river dolphins.

The spinosaurids probably did not rely on a fish diet, and it would be unreasonable for a *Spinosaurus*, as big as a *Tyrannosaurus*, to feed exclusively on such small prey. Stomach contents, and the presence of spinosaurid teeth in the bones of other animals, suggest that they may have fed on land-living animals too. The big claw may have been a killing weapon, but the specialized teeth seem to have been unsuited for hunting. The spinosaurids probably filled out their fish diet with the carrion of dead animals.

Irritator

The name of this dinosaur is derived from the frustration felt by British palaeontologist Dave Martill when faced with the skull. When it was obtained from Brazil it had been doctored by the finder to try to make it look more spectacular and marketable. After it had been prepared properly, it was seen to be the skull of a spinosaurid.

Features: Only the skull of *Irritator* is known, but it obviously came from a spinosaurid. It is the only one known from South America, although another, *Angaturama*, has been described. *Angaturama*, however, is generally regarded as another name for *Irritator*. In 2004, Eric Buffetaut found the tooth of a spinosaurid, probably *Irritator*, embedded in the backbone of a Brazilian pterosaur, suggesting that the diet of these animals was not confined to fish.

Distribution: Brazil.
Classification: Theropoda, Spinosauridae.
Meaning of name: Irritator.
Named by: Martill, Cruikshank, Frey, Small and Clarke, 1996.
Time: Albian stage of the early Cretaceous.
Size: 8m (26ft).
Lifestyle: Fish hunter, predator or scavenger.
Species: *I. challengeri* (also *Angaturama* which is not valid).

Left: The specific name I. challengeri *(illustrated) refers to Professor Challenger, the hero of Sir Arthur Conan Doyle's novel* The Lost World *in which live dinosaurs are found existing in South America.*

ABELISAURIDS

In late Cretaceous times the continents had split up and the various landmasses were drifting away from each other. This meant that different groups of dinosaurs began to develop in different parts of the world. The abelisaurids represent the big, heavy-bodied meat-eating dinosaurs that existed in the southern continents – South America, Africa and Madagascar.

Aucasaurus

Known from an almost complete skeleton, lacking only the end of the tail, *Aucasaurus* was found in lake sediments in Patagonia in 1999. This makes it the best-known abelisaurid skeleton, and it is used as the basis for several other reconstructions. There was damage to the skull of the skeleton found, suggesting that this individual had been involved in a fight shortly before its death.

Features: *Aucasaurus* is similar to its relative, *Carnotaurus*, but only about two-thirds the size. Where *Carnotaurus* has horns on the sides of its head, *Aucasaurus* only has bumps, probably used as sexual display structures. The arms, although tiny, are not as small as those of *Carnotaurus*, and seem to be made up of all humerus, the bones of the lower arm being hardly larger than those of the four fingers.

Distribution: Neuquen Province, Argentina.
Classification: Theropoda, Neoceratosauria, Abelisauria.
Meaning of name: Lizard from Auca Mahuevo.
Named by: Chiappe and Coria, 2001.
Time: Campanian stage of the late Cretaceous.
Size: 5m (16½ft).
Lifestyle: Hunter.
Species: *A. garridoi*.

Carnotaurus

An almost complete skeleton of *Carnotaurus* was extracted with difficulty from the hard mineral nodule in which it was preserved in Argentina. The deep skull suggests that it may have had an acute sense of smell, but the strength of the jaws and neck implied by the muscle attachments seem at odds with the weakness of the lower jaw and the teeth.

Features: The head is very short and squashed-looking with a shallow, hooked lower jaw. Two horns stick out sideways from above the eyes, probably being used for sparring with rivals. The arms are

Distribution: Argentina.
Classification: Theropoda, Neoceratosauria, Abelisauria.
Meaning of name: Flesh-eating bull.
Named by: Bonaparte, 1985.
Time: Campanian to Maastrichtian stage of the late Cretaceous.
Size: 7.5m (25ft).
Lifestyle: Hunter.
Species: *C. sastrei*.

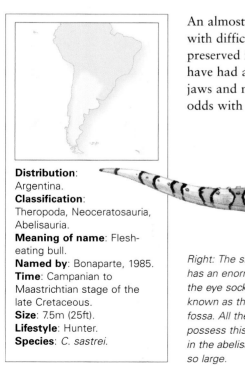

Right: The skull of Carnotaurus *has an enormous hole in front of the eye sockets; this is known as the antorbital fossa. All theropods possess this, but only in the abelisaurids is it so large.*

extremely short with no apparent forearms, even shorter than the tiny arms of *Tyrannosaurus*. They form mere stumps with four miniscule fingers. The skin texture, the best-known of any theropod, has a groundmass of small, pebbly scales but with large, conical scutes forming rows along the sides.

OVIRAPTORIDS AND THERIZINOSAURIDS

As the Cretaceous period drew on, many theropods became bird-like, with coverings of feathers that indicated a warm-blooded metabolism and active lifestyle. They developed specializations for tackling a wider range of foodstuffs. The oviraptorids had short powerful beaks with no teeth, possibly for eating eggs, shellfish or hard plant material like nuts. The therizinosaurs were plant-eaters.

Oviraptor

Distribution: Mongolia.
Classification: Theropoda, Tetanurae, Coelurosauria, Oviraptorosauria.
Meaning of name: Egg stealer.
Named by: Ostrom, 1924.
Time: Campanian stage of the late Cretaceous.
Size: 1.8m (6ft).
Lifestyle: Specialist feeder.
Species: *O. philoceratops, O. mongoliensis.*

The genus name *Oviraptor* derives from the belief that the first *Oviraptor* found had been eating the eggs of a ceratopsian dinosaur. The mouth seems to have evolved for a crushing action, and the current diet suggestions point to shellfish or nuts. There seems to be a variation in size and shape of the skull crest, maybe a sign of different stages of growth and maturity, or different species. The skull, on which most restorations, including this one, are based, is thought to have belonged to the related oviraptorid *Citipati*.

Right: Oviraptor *hands are very long. Its eggs are about the size of a hot-dog bun.*

Features: As with all other oviraptorids the head is short and carries a heavy toothless beak at the end of its well-muscled jaws. A hollow crest, like that of a cassowary, which sticks up on the head was probably used for display and intimidation. There is a pair of teeth on the palate. The skull is extremely lightweight and has very large eye sockets.

Khaan

The three almost complete articulated skeletons that have been excavated give a good idea of what this oviraptorid looked like. It was first thought to have been a specimen of the related oviraptorid, *Ingenia*, showing just how little variation there was between animals of this group. Several oviraptorids lived in the same area at the same time. The specific name of the type species *K. mckennai* honours American palaeontologist Malcolm McKenna.

Features: *Khaan* has a short and compact skull that lacks the crest possessed by *Oviraptor* and some of its relatives. It differs from the others of the group mostly by differences in the structure of the hand and the structure of the skull, which is rather more primitive. This is one of the smaller oviraptorids, but it has the same specialized head, long neck, huge hands, big feet and short tail.

Left: We have a good idea of the appearance of Khaan *because of the completeness of the skeletons found. Such detail allows us to restore the appearance of others of the group that are not so complete.*

Distribution: Ukhaa Tolgod, Mongolia.
Classification: Theropoda, Tetanurae, Coelurosauria, Oviraptorosauria.
Meaning of name: Asian warlord.
Named by: Clark, Norell and Barsbold, 2001.
Time: Campanian stage of the late Cretaceous.
Size: 1.2m (4ft).
Lifestyle: Specialist feeder.
Species: *K. mckennai.*

Nothronychus

Most therizinosaurid are Asian. The first to be found outside Asia is the most complete. It lived at the edge of the shallow sea that covered most of central North America at the time, in swampy deltas in the area of the Arizona/New Mexico borderlands. It is one of the few dinosaurs to be found from the early part of the late Cretaceous. Its name comes from the similarity between it and the giant ground sloths that existed until a few million years ago.

Distribution: New Mexico, USA.
Classification: Theropoda, Tetanurae, Coelurosauria, Therizinosauria.
Meaning of name: Sloth claw.
Named by: Kirkland and Wolfe vide Stanley, 2001.
Time: Turonian stage of the late Cretaceous.
Size: 4.5–6m (15–18½ ft).
Lifestyle: Unclear.
Species: *N. mckinleyi*.

Right: The resemblance to a ground sloth lies in its upright stance and the enormous claws on its hands. The claws were probably used for pulling down vegetation in the swampy forests where it lived.

Features: The almost complete skeleton of this animal forms the basis for most modern restorations of therizinosaurids. It has a small head on a long neck, leaf-shaped teeth (suggesting a herbivorous habit), a heavy body with broad hips (also suggesting a partial diet of plant material), heavy hands and a short, stumpy tail. It carried itself with a more upright stance than other theropods, and its hind legs are relatively short. The hip girdle has the swept-back bird-like ischium bone that is usually only seen in plant-eating dinosaurs.

THERIZINOSAUR DIET

With heads containing leaf-shaped, plant-shredding teeth, cheek pouches (indicated by the depressions at the side of the head), sharp cutting beaks, huge ripping claws and heavy, pot-bellied bodies, the therizinosaurids' lifestyle has always been a mystery. The hip bones, although in most respects saurischian, have the swept-back pubis typical of the ornithischians. This could be an adaptation to a plant-eating diet, to accommodate the big plant-processing digestive system.

However, we see this feature also in the dromaeosaurids – as unambiguous a family of meat-eaters as we can find.

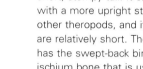

One intriguing interpretation of the huge claws is a comparison with the big claws of modern ant-eating animals, such as ant-eaters, aardvarks, armadillos and the like. In these animals the claws are an adaptation to ripping into nests and logs to reach tiny insects. However, it seems unlikely that such a diet would support an animal as big as *Therizinosaurus*.

The most likely interpretation is that the therizinosaurs were plant-eaters, the huge claws being used for ripping branches down from trees. What environmental pressures induced a family of meat-eating theropods to evolve into such a lifestyle is still a mystery.

Neimongosaurus

Neimongosaurus is known from two partial skeletons, one of which has most of the backbone and nearly all the limb bones. We know of only part of the skull, including the brain box. Mysterious arm and claw bones found in the same area in 1920, and named *Alectrosaurus*, may belong to *Neimongosaurus* and shed light on the missing hand bones.

Features: The long neck and the short tail, as well as the air spaces in the vertebrae and the arrangement of the shoulder muscles, suggest that these animals are closely related to the oviraptorids. Unfortunately, the hand bones are absent and we cannot compare them with the rest of the group. The jaw is deep and markedly down-turned, and bears a broad beak. The teeth are very similar to those of some ornithischians, suggesting a plant diet.

Distribution: Nei Mongol, China.
Classification: Theropoda, Tetanurae, Coelurosauria, Therizinosauria.
Meaning of name: Lizard from Nei Mongol.
Named by: Xu, Sereno, Kuang and Tan, 2001.
Time: Cenomanian to Campanian stages of the late Cretaceous.
Size: 2.3m (7½ ft).
Lifestyle: Unclear.
Species: *N. yangi*.

Left: The shoulder girdle is very much like that of an oviraptorid, as are the vertebrae, which are full of air spaces.

DROMAEOSAURIDS

Without a doubt the dromaeosaurids were the most important active predators of late Cretaceous times.
With their clawed hands that could grasp prey between their palms, their killing claw on the hind foot,
and their mental agility that would have enabled them to balance and slash at the same time, they
represented a fearsome group of animals.

Dromaeosaurus

Distribution: Alberta, Canada, and Montana, USA.
Classification: Theropoda, Tetanurae, Coelurosauria, Deinonychosauria.
Meaning of name: Running lizard.
Named by: Matthew and Brown, 1922.
Time: Campanian stage.
Size: 1.8m (6ft).
Lifestyle: Hunter.
Species: *D. albertensis*, *D. cristatus*, *D. gracilis*, *D. explanatus*.

Dromaeosaurus was the first of the group to have been discovered, and led to the establishment of the family. It is surprisingly poorly known, although a cast of a complete mounted skeleton, prepared by the Tyrrell Museum in Alberta, Canada, appears in several museums throughout the world. Its construction was made possible by knowledge of others of the group that have been discovered more recently.

Left: The famous dinosaur hunter Barnum Brown found the first and best of the Dromaeosaurus remains on the banks of the Red Deer River in Alberta, Canada, in 1914, naming it eight years later.

Features: The jaws are long and heavily built, and the neck is curved and flexible. The snout is deep and rounded. The tail is stiff and straight, articulated only at the base, stiffened by bony rods growing backwards from above and below the individual vertebrae. This would have helped the animal to balance while hunting prey. Its large eyes gave it excellent vision, and the size of the nasal cavities suggest that it could hunt by smell as well. The killing claw on the second toe is smaller than that of others of the group, but still efficient.

Saurornitholestes

This hunting dinosaur is known from the remains of three individuals. One remarkable occurrence is of a *Saurornitholestes*' tooth embedded in a pterosaur bone. It is not impossible to imagine an active predator like this snatching a pterosaur from the sky, but it is more likely that it scavenged the carcass of a pterosaur that had already died.

Features: The shape of the skull suggests a bigger brain than many of its relatives, but a poorer sense of smell. The teeth are also different from those of *Dromaeosaurus*, but otherwise the two animals are very similar, having grasping hands with sharp claws and a killing claw on the second toe. It was originally classed among the troodontids, but now some palaeontologists regard it as a species of *Velociraptor*.

Distribution: Alberta, Canada.
Classification: Theropoda, Tetanurae, Coelurosauria, Deinonychosauria.
Meaning of name: Lizard bird thief.
Named by: Sues, 1978.
Time: Campanian stage of the late Cretaceous.
Size: 2m (6½ft).
Lifestyle: Hunter.
Species: *S. langstoni*.

Right: Saurornitholestes seems to be an amalgam of different animals. The head is very much like that of Velociraptor, *while the rest of the skeleton (what has been found of it) is more like that of* Deinonychus.

TYRANNOSAURIDS

At the end of the Age of Dinosaurs, the biggest of the meat-eaters of the Northern Hemisphere were the tyrannosaurids. By then, their body shape had settled into a consistent design, with each of the late examples becoming almost indistinguishable from the others. In the Northern Hemisphere they occupied the ecological niches that were occupied by the abelisaurids in the south.

Tyrannosaurus

Perhaps the best-known of all dinosaurs, *Tyrannosaurus* held the record for the biggest and most powerful land-living predator of all time for a century, until the discovery of the big allosaurids, such as *Carcharodontosaurus* and *Giganotosaurus*, in the 1990s. About 20 skeletons of *Tyrannosaurus* are known, some articulated and some scattered, and so the appearance of this dinosaur is known with confidence.

Features: The skull is short and deep, and solid compared with that of other big meat-eaters. The teeth are 8–16cm (3–6in) long and about 2.5cm (1in) wide. Those at the front are D-shaped, built for gripping, while the back teeth are thin blades, evolved for shearing meat. The eyes are positioned so that they give a stereoscopic view forward. The ear structure is like that of crocodiles, which have good hearing.

Distribution: Alberta to Texas, USA.
Classification: Theropoda, Tetanurae, Coelurosauria, Tyrannosauroidea.
Meaning of name: Tyrant lizard.
Named by: Osborn, 1905.
Time: Maastrichtian stage of the late Cretaceous.
Size: 12m (39ft).
Lifestyle: Hunter or scavenger.
Species: *T. rex*, although *Daspletosaurus*, *Gorgosaurus* and *Tarbosaurus* are sometimes regarded as species of *Tyrannosaurus*.

Tarbosaurus

Tyrannosaurid *Tarbosaurus* is the largest Asian predator known, a close cousin of *Tyrannosaurus*. Indeed some regard it as a species of *Tyrannosaurus*, named *T. bataar*. Three skeletons were found by a Russian expedition to the Nemegt Formation, in the Gobi Desert, in the 1940s. Since then there have been almost as many *Tarbosaurus* skeletons as *Tyrannosaurus* skeletons found.

Features: *Tarbosaurus* is very similar to *Tyrannosaurus*, but it is less heavily built. It has a larger head with a shallower snout and lower jaw, and slightly smaller teeth. The other differences are in minor points of the shape of the

Distribution: China and Mongolia.
Classification: Theropoda, Tetanurae, Coelurosauria, Tyrannosauroidea.
Meaning of name: Alarming lizard.
Named by: Maleev, 1955.
Time: Maastrichtian stage of the late Cretaceous.
Size: 12m (39ft).
Lifestyle: Hunter or scavenger.
Species: *T. efremovi*, *T. bataar*.

individual skull bones. These features are slightly more primitive in *Tarbosaurus*, and so the early evolution may have taken place in Asia. Had it been found in North America, *Tarbosaurus* would have been regarded as a species of *Tyrannosaurus*.

Right: The two Tarbosaurus *skeletons found in Mongolia in the 1940s are currently mounted in the Palaeontological Institute of the Russian Academy of Sciences in Moscow, Russia.*

PROSAUROPODS

The first of the big, long-necked plant-eaters were the prosauropods. These ranged from turkey-sized animals to lumbering beasts that resembled the gigantic sauropods to come. Most moved about on their hind legs but the largest would have spent their time on all fours. They existed from the late Triassic period and still existed in the early Jurassic alongside the sauropods, which eventually replaced them.

Anchisaurus

Though discovered in 1818 *Anchisaurus* was not recognized as a dinosaur until 1885. The two known species may actually represent the male and female versions of the same, with the larger being the female. It was originally thought to have been a Triassic contemporary of *Plateosaurus*, but in the 1970s the New England sandstones in which the fossil was found were proved to be Jurassic in age.

Features: If *Plateosaurus* is the classic example of the biggest medium-size prosauropod, then *Anchisaurus* is the best-known of the smallest medium-size prosauropods. It has the long neck and tail, and a slim body, with long hind legs that allowed it to walk on all fours or with its forelimbs off the ground. The teeth are bigger and the jaw mechanism stronger than those of *Plateosaurus*, suggesting that it ate tougher food.

Left: Between its discovery in 1818 and its proper identification in 1885, this animal lived under a number of names, including Megadactylus *and* Amphisaurus, *both of which were pre-occupied.*

Distribution: Connecticut and Massachusetts, USA.
Classification: Sauropodomorpha, Prosauropoda, Anchosauridae.
Meaning of name: Near lizard.
Named by: Marsh, 1885.
Time: Pliensbachian to Toarcian stages of the Jurassic.
Size: 2.5m (8ft).
Lifestyle: Low browser.
Species: *A. major*, *A. polyzelus*.

Jingshanosaurus

This is one of the best-known of the Chinese prosauropods, and is known from a complete skeleton. It is named after the town of Jingshan, or Golden Hill, in Lufeng province, China, close to where the skeleton was found. This town is the site of the Museum of Lufeng Dinosaurs, one of several big dinosaur museums in China.

Features: The complete skeleton shows *Jingshanosaurus* to be a typical large prosauropod, with a heavy body, long neck and tail, and legs that would have allowed a bipedal or quadrupedal mode of travel. It has the characteristic big sauropod claw on the thumb. The skeleton looks like a particularly large version of *Yunnanosaurus*: it may well be the same animal.

Distribution: China.
Classification: Sauropodomorpha, Prosauropoda, Massospondylidae.
Meaning of name: Lizard from Golden Hill.

Named by: Zhang and Young, 1995.
Time: Early Jurassic.
Size: 9.8m (32ft).
Lifestyle: High browser.
Species: *J. dinwaensis*.

Left: Although Jingshanosaurus *was a typical prosauropod with the typical prosauropod dentition and presumably vegetarian diet, its describers have suggested that it may have eaten molluscs as well.*

DIPLODOCIDS

If the macronarians (the brachiosaurids and camarasaurids) went for height to be impressive, the diplodocids went for length. Among these sauropods we find the longest land animals that ever existed. The slimness of the neck and tail meant that, despite its length, a diplodocid was not a particularly heavy animal. The tail was twice the length of the body and neck together, and ended in a whiplash.

Diplodocus

The familiar long, low sauropod is known as *Diplodocus*. It is well known from the many casts of the graceful skeleton of *D. carnegii*, the second species to be found. The casts, which appear in museums throughout the world, were excavated, reproduced and donated with finance provided by the Scottish-American steel magnate Andrew Carnegie in the early years of the twentieth century.

Features: The neck and tail are finely balanced around the hips and, as a result, *Diplodocus* could probably have raised itself on to its hind legs to reach high into the trees. The wear on the teeth shows that it could browse high in the treetops or among the undergrowth.

Finds in the 1990s have led American palaeontologist Steven Czerkas to suggest that there may have been a row of horny spines down the neck, back and tail.

Distribution: Colorado, Utah and Wyoming, USA.
Classification: Sauropoda, Diplodocidae.
Meaning of name: Double beam.
Named by: Marsh, 1878.
Time: Kimmeridgian to Tithonian stages of the late Jurassic.
Size: 27m (89ft).
Lifestyle: Low or high browser.
Species: *D. longus*, *D. carnegiei*, *D. hayi*.

Supersaurus

The dinosaur *Supersaurus* was one of the big sauropods found in the Dry Mesa Quarry, Colorado, by dinosaur hunter Jim Jensen. Unfortunately that site is such a jumble – probably representing a log-jam of bones in a Morrison Formation river – that the skeletons are all mixed up. One of Jensen's giants (then called *Ultrasaurus*) actually consisted of a shoulder blade of *Brachiosaurus* and ribs from *Supersaurus*.

Features: The vertebrae and the partial shoulder and hip that have been found of this animal show that it is closely related to *Diplodocus*. It may even be a large species of *Diplodocus* that stood 8m (26ft) high at the shoulder. The tallest vertebrae are as tall as a standing child. There are even bigger bones from Dry Mesa in the basement of Brigham Young University, in Salt Lake City, USA, that are yet to be examined and could alter our interpretation of what this dinosaur looked like.

Distribution: Colorado, USA.
Classification: Sauropoda, Diplodocidae.

Meaning of name: Super lizard.
Named by: Jensen, 1985.
Time: Kimmeridgian to Tithonian stages of the late Jurassic.
Size: 30m (98ft).
Lifestyle: Low or high browser.
Species: *S. vivianae*.

Right: The body proportions are based on those of Diplodocus *to which* Supersaurus *is obviously related. However, the neck may be longer than that of* Diplodocus.

MACRONARIA

The macronaria are the sauropods with the boxy heads. The distinctive head shape was due to the fact that the holes in the skull representing the nostrils were much bigger than the eye sockets. And since the nostrils were on top of the head, it is easy to see why the rather strange-looking skull has been the subject of a great deal of scientific speculation.

It was once thought that the high nostril meant that the animal could remain submerged in a lake and breathe without any of its body showing. That idea has been dismissed. Some scientists drew attention to the fact that the nostrils on an elephant's skull are extremely large as well, and that maybe these sauropods had an elephant-like trunk. But this does not make much sense, since, with a long neck, the added reach of a trunk would seem to be superfluous. Anyway, a sauropod's skull lacks the broad plates of bone that would be needed to anchor the muscles that make up a trunk.

The most likely hypothesis is that the big nasal cavities would have been filled with moist membranes in life, and would have kept the interior of the skull and the little brain cool under the hot sun that would have beaten down on the late Jurassic plains of North America.

Brachiosaurus

The best-known *Brachiosaurus* skeleton in the world is now thought to be a different genus – *Giraffatitan*. However, an even bigger animal, *Ultrasauros*, found in the Dry Mesa Quarry in Colorado, is now regarded as a particularly big specimen of *Brachiosaurus*. The original *Brachiosaurus* was discovered as two partial skeletons in the Morrison Formation near Fruita in Utah in 1900 by Elmer G. Riggs.

Distribution: Colorado and Utah, USA.
Classification: Sauropoda, Macronaria.
Meaning of name: Arm lizard.
Named by: Riggs, 1903.
Time: Kimmeridgian to Tithonian stages.
Size: 22m (72ft).
Lifestyle: High browser.
Species: *B. altithorax*.

Left: The position of the neck whether it was vertical or horizontal – is an on-going debate among scientists.

Features: About half of the height of *Brachiosaurus* is due to the neck. This, with its long front legs and tall shoulders, meant that it could reach high up into the trees to feed. Even its front feet contributed to its high reach – the fingers are long and pillar-like, and arranged vertically in the hand. Despite its fame, it is one of the rarest of the sauropods from the Morrison Formation.

Camarasaurus

This must have been one of the most abundant of the Morrison Formation sauropods, judging by the number of remains found. It is often thought of as a small animal. This is because the best skeleton found is of a juvenile, perfectly articulated, lying in the rock of Dinosaur National Monument in Utah, USA, and mounted in Pittsburgh Museum.

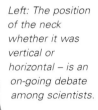

Features: The "chambered lizard" in its name refers to the cavities in the backbone, designed to keep down the weight of the animal. Other cavities are present in the skull, which is merely a framework of bony struts, with enormous nostrils and spoon-shaped teeth. The forelimbs and hind limbs are approximately the same length, making the back of the animal horizontal. It is the Morrison Formation sauropod that is less bulky than *Brachiosaurus*, but not as slim as *Diplodocus*.

Distribution: New Mexico to Montana, USA.
Classification: Sauropoda, Macronaria.
Meaning of name: Chambered lizard.
Named by: Cope, 1877.
Time: Kimmeridgian to Tithonian stages of the late Jurassic.
Size: 20m (66ft).
Lifestyle: Browser.
Species: *C. supremus, C. grandis, C. lentus, C. lewisi.*

TITANOSAURIDS

The titanosaurids were the sauropod group that dominated the Cretaceous, after the diplodocids and macronarians had become extinct. They ranged from the true titanosaurids of South America to the dwarf species of the European islands. Although a complete skull was not identified until recently, the variation of shapes in isolated skull bones suggests that different titanosaurids had different head shapes.

Hypselosaurus

The dinosaur *Hypselosaurus* is known from the scattered remains of at least ten individuals. Fossilized eggs, approximately 30cm (12in) in diameter and lying in groups of five, found near Aix in southern France (eggs-en-Provence, as some wit put it), have been attributed to *Hypselosaurus*, although this has not been scientifically confirmed. Another theory is that the eggs actually belong to a contemporary flightless bird, *Gargantuavis*.

Distribution: France and Spain.
Classification: Sauropoda, Macronaria, Titanosauria.
Meaning of name: High ridge lizard.
Named by: Matheron, 1869.
Time: Maastrichtian stage of the late Cretaceous.
Size: 12m (39ft).
Lifestyle: Browser.
Species: *H. priscus*.

Right: Hypselosaurus' *eggs are spherical, more than twice the size of ostrich eggs and have a volume of 2 litres (½ gallon).*

Features: It is difficult to restore *Hypselosaurus*. It is a large, four-footed, long-necked plant-eater, of a typical sauropod shape, and is known only from disarticulated remains. Comparing it with other titanosaurids, it seems to have had more robust limbs than its relatives. The teeth are weak and peg-shaped. We do not know whether it was covered in armour like some titanosaurids.

Magyarosaurus

The smallest known adult sauropod, *Magyarosaurus*, was found in Romania and Hungary. In late Cretaceous times this area of Europe was an island chain, and it seems likely that dwarf dinosaurs evolved on these islands to make the best use of limited food supplies. Other contemporary dwarf dinosaurs from this area include the duckbill, *Telmatosaurus*, and the ankylosaur, *Struthiosaurus*.

Below: Ampelosaurus, a *relative of* Magyarosaurus.

Features: *Magyarosaurus* is probably related to *Ampelosaurus*, and is probably one of the armoured forms. Its unusual stature makes it difficult to classify. Some scientists believe it to be a small species of '*Titanosaurus*', or even of *Hypselosaurus*, rather than a genus in its own right. In fact, the several specimens known are not consistent, and there are those with slender humeri and those with robust humeri. This may be a sexual difference, or there may be more than one genus of dwarf sauropod represented.

Distribution: Romania, Hungary.
Classification: Sauropoda, Macronaria, Titanosauria.
Meaning of name: Lizard of the Magyars, an ancient European tribe.
Named by: von Huene, 1932.
Time: Maastrichtian stage of the late Cretaceous.
Size: 6m (19½ft).
Lifestyle: Low browser.
Species: *M. dacus, M. transylvanicus*.

LITTLE ORNITHOPODS

The early plant-eating ornithopods were small, beaver-sized animals. By the early Jurassic period some had not yet evolved the cheek pouches and the chewing teeth of the later forms, but one group, the heterodontosaurids, had developed a very strange, almost mammal-like arrangement of differently sized teeth. The remains of these animals are known from desert deposits of southern Africa.

Lesothosaurus

The most primitive ornithischians, such as *Lesothosaurus*, had not evolved the complex chewing mechanism that was to characterize the later forms. Instead, they would have crushed their food by a simple up and down chopping action of the jaws. This is quite an unspecialized feeding method, and these animals may well have eaten carrion or insects as well as plants in order to survive.

Features: *Lesothosaurus* is one of the most primitive of the ornithischians, and as such it is difficult to put into a strict classification. It is a small, two-footed plant-eater, built for speed. The head, on the end of a flexible

neck, is short, triangular in profile, with big eyes. The teeth are arranged in a simple row and, unlike all other ornithopods, the mouth does not seem to have cheeks. The jaw action is one of simple chopping. The snout ends with a horn-covered, vegetation-cropping beak.

Distribution: Lesotho, South Africa.
Classification: Ornithischia, Fabrosauridae.
Meaning of name: Lizard from Lesotho.
Named by: Galton, 1978.
Time: Hettangian to Sinemurian stages of the early Jurassic.
Size: 1m (3ft).
Lifestyle: Low browser.
Species: *L. diagnosticus*.

Right: Lesothosaurus *is very similar to the earlier-discovered* Fabrosaurus. *However the* Fabrosaurus *material is so poor it is impossible to make direct comparisons. If they are the same genus, then the name* Fabrosaurus *would have to take precedence, being applied first.*

Abrictosaurus

The name of the "wide-awake lizard" derives from a dispute between palaeontologists. Tony Thulborn proposed that the heterodontosaurids slept away the hot desert summer as some modern animals do. J. A. Hopson disagreed with this theory, based on the study of the growth of the teeth, and celebrated his notion of a year-round active animal by giving this new dinosaur an appropriate name.

Features: Our knowledge of *Abrictosaurus* is based on two skulls and some fragmentary pieces of the skeleton. The skulls are almost identical to those of *Heterodontosaurus*, with a similar varied arrangement of teeth, except that they lack the prominent tusks. The remains may, in fact, represent female specimens of *Heterodontosaurus*. It is possible that only the males had the tusks and used them for

Distribution: Lesotho, South Africa.
Classification: Ornithischia, Heterodontosauridae.
Meaning of name: Wide-awake lizard.
Named by: Hopson, 1975.
Time: Hettangian to Sinemurian stages of the early Jurassic.
Size: 1.2m (4ft).
Lifestyle: Herbivore.
Species: *A. consors*.

Right: Only the skull and a few bones of Abrictosaurus *are known, and so the remainder of the restoration is based on the skeleton of* Heterodontosaurus.

display, as with many modern animals. On the other hand, many modern animal groups, such as the pigs, have prominent tusks in some genera but not in others. A wild boar's differ from those of a warthog.

IGUANODONTIDS

If the sauropods were the principal Jurassic plant-eaters, they were replaced in the early Cretaceous by the ornithopods. The iguanodontids were the most important and widespread of these. The smallest had the typical two-footed plant-eater shape and scampered around on their hind legs. The larger and more typical members of the group were too heavy for two feet and so were basically four-footed animals.

Iguanodon

Famed as being one of the first dinosaurs to be scientifically recognized, *Iguanodon* became something of a wastebasket taxon over the years. It was thought to have been a four-footed, rhinoceros-like animal until complete skeletons were found in a mine, in Belgium, in the 1880s. Thereafter, it was restored in a kangaroo-like pose. Now it is largely regarded as a four-footed animal once more.

Features: *Iguanodon* is the archetypal ornithopod. Its head is narrow and beaked, with tough, grinding teeth. Its hands consist of three weight-bearing fingers with hooves. It has a massive spike on the first finger used for defence or gathering food, and a prehensile fifth finger that works like a thumb. The hind legs are heavy and the three toes are weight-bearing. The long, deep tail balanced the animal as it walked.

Left: Although Iguanodon *was found and named by Mantell in 1825, the description was based only on teeth. In 2000 the International Commission on Zoological Nomenclature ruled the type species to be* I. bernissartensis *described in 1881, based on complete skeletons from Belgium.*

Distribution: England, Belgium, Germany and Spain.
Classification: Ornithopods, Iguanodontia.
Meaning of name: Iguana tooth.
Named by: Boulenger and van Beneden, 1881.
Time: Barremian and Valanginian stages of the early Cretaceous.
Size: 6–10m (19½–33ft).
Lifestyle: Browser.
Species: *I. bernissartensis, I. anglicus, I. atherfieldensis, I. dawsoni, I. fittoni, I. hoggi, I. lakotaensis, I. ottingeri.*

Altirhinus

Once regarded as a species of *Iguanodon* and called *I. orientalis*, there are enough differences to place *Altirhinus* in a genus of its own. It is known from five partial skeletons and two skulls, which are preserved in enough detail to show the distinctive features. It may represent an intermediate stage between the iguanodontids and the hadrosaurids.

Below: Altirhinus *looked just like* Iguanodon *except for the tall nasal region on the head.*

Features:
Altirhinus, as its name suggests, has a very high nasal region on the skull. This may have been an adaptation to an enhanced sense of smell. It had a greater number of teeth than *Iguanodon*, which provided it with a more efficient food-gathering technique. The beak is wider and flatter than that of *Iguanodon*, rather more like that of one of the later hadrosaurids. It retains the thumb spike, so distinctive of *Iguanodon* and its relatives.

Distribution: East Gobi Province, Mongolia.
Classification: Ornithopoda, Iguanodontia, Hadrosauridae.
Meaning of name: High nose.
Named by: Norman, 1998.
Time: Aptian and Albian stages of the Cretaceous.
Size: 8m (26ft).
Lifestyle: Browser.
Species: *A. kurzanovi.*

LATE CRETACEOUS ORNITHOPODS

The late Cretaceous period was the time of the big ornithopods such as the duckbilled hadrosaurids – some of which had flat heads and broad beaks, and some of which had flamboyant crests. However, there were still many smaller types that scampered around the feet of the giants. Some retained their primitive features from earlier times, but some were quite advanced.

Thescelosaurus

The classification of *Thescelosaurus*, known from complete and articulated remains, has been moved between the hypsilophodontids and the iguanodontids for most of the last century, and the authorities are still not sure where it sits. One specimen, nicknamed Willo, has the remains of the internal organs, including the heart, preserved. Its rather primitive structure is surprising considering it is among the last of the dinosaurs to have lived.

Distribution: Alberta, Canada, Saskatchewan, Colorado, Montana, South Dakota and Wyoming, USA.
Classification: Ornithopoda.
Meaning of name: Wonderful lizard.
Named by: Gilmore, 1913.
Time: Campanian to Maastrichtian stages of the late Cretaceous.
Size: 4m (13ft).
Lifestyle: Browser.
Species: *T. neglectus*. Several others, all unnamed.

Above: The specific name, Thescelosaurus neglectus, refers to the fact that the skeleton was not studied for 22 years after it was discovered and collected.

Features: *Thescelosaurus* is more heavily built than other medium-sized ornithopods, and the legs are relatively shorter. This is not an animal built for speed. As with its relatives, it has a beak at the front of the mouth but an unusual arrangement of three different kinds of teeth – sharp in the front, canine-like at the side and molar-like grinding teeth at the back. The four-toed foot is one of the primitive features of *Thescelosaurus*.

Orodromeus

Skeletons of this small ornithopod were found in Montana with the remains of dinosaur eggs and nests at a site known as Egg Mountain. For some time it was believed that *Orodromeus* was the builder of the nests, but later it was found that they actually belonged to the meat-eater *Troodon* and that *Orodromeus* represented the prey.

Features: This is a fairly primitive small ornithopod. Its legs show it to have been a speedy animal, hence its name. The head is small, with a beak and cheek pouches. The neck is long and flexible, and the tail is stiffened by bony rods that helped to keep it straight for balance while running. There are three toes on the hind foot, and four fingers on the hand.

Distribution: Montana, USA.
Classification: Ornithopoda.
Meaning of name: Mountain runner.
Named by: Horner and Weishampel, 1988.
Time: Campanian stage of the late Cretaceous.
Size: 2.5m (8ft).
Lifestyle: Low browser.
Species: *O. makelai*.

Left: Fossil finds of Orodromeus *suggest that it lived in small groups.*

Parasaurolophus

Probably the most familiar lambeosaurine hadrosaurid, and the one with the most flamboyant crest, was *Parasaurolophus*. Three species are recognized, and each has a different curve of the crest. Different crest sizes may indicate different sexes. Computer studies in the New Mexico Museum of Natural History and Science have produced a deep trombone-like sound that would have been produced by *Parasaurolphus* snorting through its crest.

Distribution: New Mexico, USA, to Alberta, Canada.
Classification: Ornithopoda, Iguanodontia, Hadrosauroidea, Lambeosaurinae.
Meaning of name: Almost Saurolophus.
Named by: Parks, 1922.
Time: Campanian to Maastrichtian stages of the late Cretaceous.
Size: 10m (33ft).
Lifestyle: Browser.
Species: *P. walkeri, P. cyrtocristatus, P. tibicen.*

Features: The crest sweeps backwards from the back of the skull in a gentle curve. It consists of a convoluted series of tubes that run back from the nostril. The tip of the crest coincides with a notch in the backbone at the shoulders, giving rise to the idea that when the tip of the crest nestled in the notch, the animal presented a smooth profile and was able to push its way through thick bush.

Lambeosaurus

This is a well-known dinosaur, and gives its name to the whole group. Its remains were discovered in 1889, but it was not recognized as a distinct genus until 1923. More than 20 fossils have been found. The wide geographical range of the finds suggests that it lived all along the western shore of the late Cretaceous inland sea of North America.

Features: The hollow crest on the top of the head is in the shape of an axe, with a squarish blade sticking up and a shaft pointing backwards. The square portion is the hollow part with the convoluted nasal passages, while the spike is solid. The crest of the larger species, *L. magnicristatus*, has a larger hollow portion, bigger than the skull itself, and a very small spike. The skin is thin and covered in small polygonal scales.

Distribution: Alberta, Canada, and Montana to New Mexico, USA.
Classification: Ornithopoda, Iguanodontia, Hadrosauroidea, Lambeosaurinae.
Meaning of name: Lawrence M. Lambe's lizard.
Named by: Parks, 1923.
Time: Campanian stage of the late Cretaceous.
Size: 9–15m (30–49ft).
Lifestyle: Browser.
Species: *L. lambei, L. laticaudus, L. magnicristatus.*

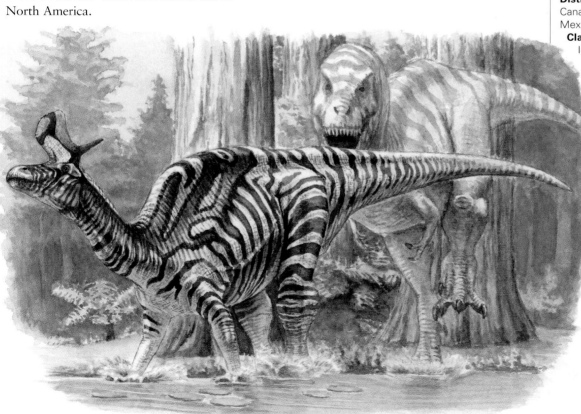

PRIMITIVE ARMOURED DINOSAURS

In early Jurassic times, a new group of dinosaurs began to appear. They were distinguished by the presence of armour on their backs, as bony plates covered in horn, embedded in the skin. Armoured dinosaurs were all plant-eaters and evolved from the ornithischian, or the bird-hipped, line. The evolutionary spur would have been the presence of so many big, contemporary, meat-eating dinosaurs.

Scutellosaurus

This plant-eating dinosaur would have sought refuge from its enemies in two different ways, either by running away, or by squatting down and letting the armour deter enemies. It had long hind legs and a very long tail for balance that would have enabled it to run. Its strong front legs would have carried its body as it hunkered down in passive defence.

Features: If it were not for the armour plates, this animal would have been regarded as a primitive ornithopod. It has the simple dentition, and the long hind legs and tail. The presence of this armour suggests that *Scutellosaurus* was close to the ancestry of the big plated and armoured dinosaurs to come. It would have evolved from purely bipedal ancestors.

Distribution: Arizona, USA.
Classification: Ornithischia, basal Thyreophora.
Meaning of name: Little shield lizard.
Named by: Colbert, 1981.
Time: Hetangian stage of the early Jurassic.
Size: 1.2m (4ft).
Lifestyle: Low browser.
Species: *S. lawleri*.

Left: The armour consists of more than 300 little shields in six different types, ranging from tiny lumps to big stegosaur-like plates.

Scelidosaurus

The first almost complete dinosaur skeleton to be discovered and named was *Scelidosaurus*. As an armoured dinosaur it would have been a slow-moving creature, but the length of its hind legs and weight of its tail seem to suggest that it may have been able to run on two legs for short distances.

Features: This very primitive animal belonged to the group known as the thyreophorans. The group consists of the plated dinosaurs (the stegosaurs) and the armoured dinosaurs (the ankylosaurs). In the past it has been regarded as ancestral to the stegosaurs, but now it is thought to be closer to the ancestors of the ankylosaurs. Its back, sides and tail are covered by an arrangement of armoured scutes with a mosaic of small armoured scales between them.

Distribution: Dorset, England.
Classification: Ornithischia, Thyreophora, Ankylosauromorpha.
Meaning of name: Leg lizard.
Named by: Owen, 1868.
Time: Sinemurian to Pliensbachian stages of the early Jurassic.
Size: 4m (13ft).
Lifestyle: Low browser.
Species: *S. harrisonii*.

Right: Two almost complete skeletons of Scelidosaurus *have been found in southern England, and it is from these skeletons that we can reconstruct the likely appearance of related, less complete, animals.*

STEGOSAURS AND ANKYLOSAURS

The stegosaurs were the plated dinosaurs of Jurassic and early Cretaceous times. They appear to have evolved in Asia – most of the primitive forms are found in China – and then migrated to North America and to Africa. The ankylosaurs had armour that consisted of bony plates forming a pavement covering the back. Defence consisted of sideways pointing spikes or a club at the end of the tail.

Stegosaurus

Although *S. armatus* was the first stegosaurus species to be found, *S. stenops*, found by Othniel Charles Marsh, is the more familiar species. The back plates were once thought to have been

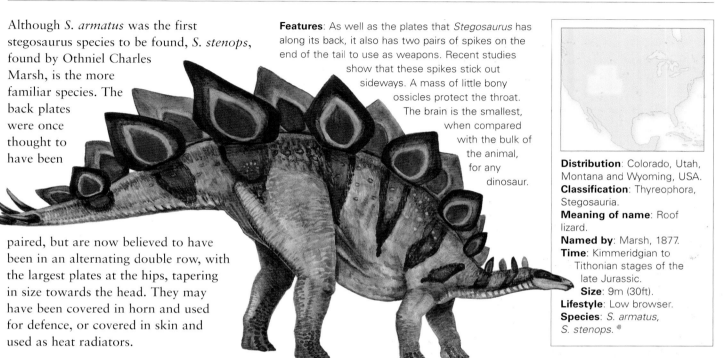

paired, but are now believed to have been in an alternating double row, with the largest plates at the hips, tapering in size towards the head. They may have been covered in horn and used for defence, or covered in skin and used as heat radiators.

Features: As well as the plates that *Stegosaurus* has along its back, it also has two pairs of spikes on the end of the tail to use as weapons. Recent studies show that these spikes stick out sideways. A mass of little bony ossicles protect the throat. The brain is the smallest, when compared with the bulk of the animal, for any dinosaur.

Distribution: Colorado, Utah, Montana and Wyoming, USA.
Classification: Thyreophora, Stegosauria.
Meaning of name: Roof lizard.
Named by: Marsh, 1877.
Time: Kimmeridgian to Tithonian stages of the late Jurassic.
   Size: 9m (30ft).
Lifestyle: Low browser.
Species: *S. armatus, S. stenops.*

Tuojiangosaurus

The best-known of the many Chinese stegosaurs, and the first to have been discovered is *Tuojiangosaurus*. It is known from two partial skeletons, one of which is 50 per cent complete. Its similarity to *Stegosaurus* shows that the two animals obviously had the same lifestyle and ate the same food – leafy plants growing low on the ground.

Features: *Tuojiangosaurus* has 15 pairs of small, pointed plates running down the neck, back and tail, as well as two pairs of spikes on the tail. As with all stegosaurs, it has a long head, with spoon-shaped teeth and a toothless beak. The teeth are very like those of *Stegosaurus* – small, coarsely serrated and vertically grooved.

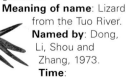

Distribution: China.
Classification: Thyreophora, Stegosauria.
   Meaning of name: Lizard from the Tuo River.
      Named by: Dong, Li, Shou and Zhang, 1973.
         Time: Kimmeridgian to Tithonian stages of the late Jurassic.
Size: 7m (23ft).
Lifestyle: Low browser.
Species: *T. multispinus.*

Left: Tuojiangosaurus *had the typical stegosaur build of an arched back and a bulky body, and walked on pillar-like limbs.*

Animantarx

This dinosaur has the distinction of being the first to be found by radiometric survey. Ramal Jones, a technician at the University of Utah, USA, knowing fossil bones to be slightly radioactive, surveyed a likely fossil site in Utah and persuaded the university to excavate the spot where low-level radiation seemed strongest.

Features: *Animantarx* is known from remains that consist of a partial skull with its jawbone, and a partial skeleton consisting of backbones, ribs, shoulder structure and parts of front and rear legs. It is a medium-size nodosaurid that resembles *Pawpawsaurus* with armour plates like upturned boats. The skull has a very high cranium and two pairs of short horns, one pair behind the eyes and another on the cheeks.

Top: Pawpawsaurus.

Left: "A 12ft-long dinosaur, looking like an armadillo but bigger than a cow," was how Don Burge, one of the team that studied Animantarx, *described it.*

Distribution: Utah, USA.
Classification: Thyreophora, Ankylosauria, Nodosauridae.
Meaning of name: Animated living fortress.
Named by: Carpenter, Kirkland, Burge and Bird, 1999.
Time: Cenomanian to Turonian stages of the late Cretaceous.
Size: 3m (10ft).
Lifestyle: Low browser.
Species: *A. ramaljonesi*.

NODOSAURIDS AND ANKYLOSAURIDS

There were two groups of ankylosaurs – nodosaurids, that defended themselves with spikes on their shoulders, and ankylosaurids, that defended themselves with clubs on their tails. The main difference between the heads of the two groups is in the breadth of the mouth. A nodosaurid tended to have a pear-shaped skull that narrowed towards the jaws, unlike the hourglass-shaped jaws of an ankylosaurid with its broad beak. At the time these dinosaurs thrived, flowering plants had evolved, and there would have been plenty of leafy and seed-bearing undergrowth to be grazed. The nodosaurids, with their narrower mouths, must have been selective in their food choices, unlike the broad-mouthed ankylosaurids.

Common to both groups is the presence of a palate in the roof of the mouth (typical in mammals but rare in dinosaurs). The palate is a shelf that separates the airways of the nostrils from the foodways of the mouth, allowing that animal to eat and breathe at the same time. This would have speeded up the eating process.

Below: The difference in the shape of the head between a nodosaurid (left) and an ankylosaurid (right) is obvious in top view.

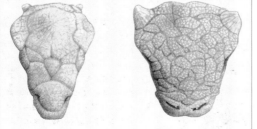

Struthiosaurus

This is the smallest known of the nodosaurids. Its remains have been found all across Europe, in areas that are known to have been parts of an island chain during late Cretaceous times. Its small stature is taken to be proof that animals on islands tend to develop dwarf forms to make the best use of limited resources.

Features: *Struthiosaurus* resembles its larger relatives, but is more lightly built. The armour consists of three pairs of sideways-projecting spikes on the neck, at least one pair of tall spines over the shoulders and a double row of triangular plates sticking up along the tail. The back is covered in keeled scutes separated by a groundmass of ossicles, and there seems to be a well-marked boundary between the armoured back and the skin of the underside.

Distribution: Austria, France and Hungary.
Classification: Thyreophora, Ankylosauria, Nodosauridae.
Meaning of name: Ostrich lizard.
Named by: Bunzel, 1871.
Time: Campanian stage of the late Cretaceous.
Size: 2m (6½ft).
Lifestyle: Low browser.
Species: *S. austriacus, S. ludgunensis, S. transylvanicus.*

PRIMITIVE ASIAN CERATOPSIANS

The main division of the marginocephalian group is represented by the ceratopsians, or ceratopians as some palaeontologists prefer. These are the horned dinosaurs. Their origin can be traced back into early Cretaceous times, but it was in the late Cretaceous period that they really came into their own. The early forms were quite graceful little animals but they soon evolved into pig-sized beasts.

Graciliceratops

When *Graciliceratops* was discovered in 1975, the skeleton was referred to as a specimen of *Microceratops gobiensis*, but Paul Sereno of Chicago subsequently identified it as the juvenile of something quite different. The name derives from its small size and light build, and its bipedal stance shows that the group had its origins in the two-footed plant-eaters.

Above: This primitive ceratopsian was evidently able to move swiftly on its hind legs, unlike its heavy successors.

Features: Although this dinosaur is only known from a juvenile skeleton, there is enough to show that it is basically a bipedal animal with a front limb that is smaller than the hind limb. The hind limbs show that it was capable of running swiftly. As with all primitive ceratopsians, it has a beak at the front of its mouth and a ridge of bone, not quite a shield, around the back of the skull.

Distribution: Omnogov, Mongolia.
Classification: Marginocephalia, Ceratopsia, Neoceratopsia.
Meaning of name: Graceful horned face.
Named by: Sereno, 2000.
Time: Santonian to Campanian stages of the late Cretaceous.
Size: 0.9m (3ft), but this is immature. The adult was probably 2m (6½ft).
Lifestyle: Low browser.
Species: *G. mongoliensis*.

Protoceratops

There have been dozens of skeletons of *Protoceratops* found, both adult and juvenile, and so the whole growth pattern is known. It was found by the expeditions to the Gobi Desert undertaken by the American Museum of Natural History in the 1920s. It seems to have lived in herds, and its remains are so abundant that it has been termed the "sheep of the Cretaceous".

Features: *Protoceratops* is a heavy animal with short legs, a deep tail and a heavy head. Although a member of the horned dinosaurs, it does not have true horns. Two forms of adult are known, a lightweight form with a low frill, and a heavier form with a big frill and a bump on the snout where a horn would have been. These probably represent the two sexes, with the males having the heavier head.

Distribution: China and Mongolia.
Classification: Marginocephalia, Ceratopsia, Neoceratopsia.
Meaning of name: Before the horned heads.
Named by: Granger and Gregory, 1923.
Time: Santonian and Campanian stages of the late Cretaceous.
Size: 2.5m (8ft).
Lifestyle: Low browser.
Species: *P. andrewsi*.

SHORT-FRILLED CERATOPSIDS

The big horned dinosaurs of the late Cretaceous period belonged to the group called the Ceratopsidae. They were only found in North America, with the possible exception of Turanosaurus *from Kazakhstan. They nearly all had massive rhinoceros-like bodies and heavy, armoured heads. They can be divided into two subgroups, the short-frilled Centrosaurinae and the long-frilled Chamosaurinae.*

Avaceratops

Although the ceratopsids are generally big animals, *Avaceratops* is quite small. It is known from an almost complete skeleton missing only the hip bones, much of the tail and, frustratingly, the roof of the skull including the horn cores. The skeleton found is not an adult, since most of the skull came apart before it fossilized, but it was almost fully grown when it died.

Features: This small ceratopsid has a short frill that is quite thick. Like other centrosaurines it has a short, deep snout, a powerful lower jaw with batteries of double-rooted shearing teeth, and a beak like that of a parrot. It is assumed that like other centrosaurines, it has a bigger horn on the nose than above the eyes. It may be a juvenile or subadult of some other genus such as *Monoclonius*.

Distribution: Montana, USA.
Classification: Marginocephalia, Ceratopsia, Ceratopsidae, Centrosaurinae.
Meaning of name: Ava's horned face (from Ava Cole, the wife of the discoverer).
Named by: Dodson, 1986.
Time: Campanian stage of the late Cretaceous.
Size: 2.5m (8ft), but this was a juvenile. The grown animal was probably 4m (13ft).
Lifestyle: Low browser.
Species: *A. lammersi.*

Right: Avaceratops *looked like a diminutive version of its giant contemporaries.*

Centrosaurus

Distribution: Alberta, Canada.
Classification: Marginocephalia, Ceratopsia, Ceratopsidae, Centrosaurinae.
Meaning of name: Pointed lizard.
Named by: Lambe, 1904.
Time: Campanian stage of the late Cretaceous.
Size: 6m (19½ft).
Lifestyle: Low browser.
Species: *C. cutleri, C. apertus.*

The animal to which the short-frilled group owes its name is known from at least 15 skulls and pieces of bone from animals of all stages of growth. The first part of the skeleton to be found was the back of the neck shield, with its hook-shaped horns which give the animal its name (not the single nose horn).

Features: *Centrosaurus* is noted for the big, single horn on its snout, as well as smaller horns over the eyes and others like hooks on the neck shield. The edge of the shield has bony growths. The big horn curves forward in some individuals, leans back in others, and yet sticks straight up in others, a variation that palaeontologists do not seem to think significant. A pair of openings, or *fenestrae*, on the neck shield keeps the weight down.

LONG-FRILLED CERATOPSIDS

The Chasmosaurinae represent the second of the two groups of advanced ceratopsians. They were also rhinoceros-sized beasts, but with long neck shields. They generally had long snouts, and the brow horns were usually bigger than the nose horn. Like the Centrosaurinae, they were confined to the North American continent where they lived in herds migrating across the open plains.

Chasmosaurus

Distribution: Alberta, Canada, to Texas, USA.
Classification: Marginocephalia, Ceratopsia, Ceratopsidae, Chasmosaurinae.
Meaning of name: Chasm reptile.
Named by: Lambe, 1904.
Time: Maastrichtian stage of the late Cretaceous.
Size: 6m (19½ft).
Lifestyle: Low browser.
Species: *C. belli, C. russelli.*

In the 1880s the dinosaur-bearing beds of Canada were being opened up. Many spectacular horned dinosaurs were found, and by the turn of the century about half-a-dozen species of the spectacularly frilled *Chasmosaurus* had been identified. More detailed study by Canadians Stephen Godfrey and Robert Holmes in 1995 whittled these species down to two.

Features: The obvious feature of *Chasmosaurus* is the vast frill, like a huge triangular sail, around the back of its head. The weight of this structure is kept to a minimum by the holes (or chasms, hence the name) that reduces it essentially to a framework of struts. In life this shield would have been covered in skin, and was probably brightly coloured to act as a display organ.

Pentaceratops

C. M. Sternberg, the professional fossil collector who did much of the early work in exploring the dinosaur beds of Canada, turned his attention to New Mexico, USA, in the 1920s. One of the first dinosaurs he found there was a ceratopsian, later named *Pentaceratops*. The narrowness of the neck shield and the pointed cheek bones distinguished this from all other horned dinosaurs so far discovered.

Features: *Pentaceratops* does not really have five horns as the name implies. The epijugal angles, that stick out of the corner of the cheek bones, are very pointed, and give the impression of an extra pair of horns, especially when the head shield is seen from the front. Distinguishing features like this would have helped individuals to identify their own herds on the highly populated plains of the time. A brightly coloured pattern on the shield would have enhanced this effect.

Distribution: New Mexico and Colorado, USA.
Classification: Marginocephalia, Ceratopsia, Ceratopsidae, Chasmosaurinae.
Meaning of name: Five-horned face.
Named by: Osborn, 1923.
Time: Campanian to Maastrichtian stages of the late Cretaceous.
Size: 6m (19½ft).
Lifestyle: Low browser.
Species: *P. sternbergi.*

GLOSSARY

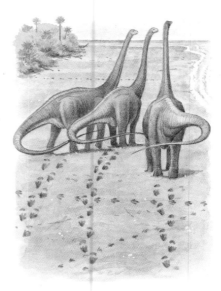

Abelisaurid A group of theropods of the late Cretaceous, mostly from the Southern Hemisphere.

Alvarezsaurid Long-legged running dinosaurs with diminutive forelimbs, often classed as primitive birds.

Amphibious A creature able to survive on land or in the water.

Ankylosaur Quadrupedal herbivorous ornithischian dinosaurs from the late Cretaceous, making up the suborder Ankylosauria.

Ankylosaurid A member of the Ankylosauridae, a family of the suborder Ankylosauria.

Antorbital fossa A hole in the skull between the snout and the eye socket.

Archosaur A member of the diapsid group of reptiles that includes the crocodiles, the pterosaurs and the dinosaurs – the so-called "ruling reptiles".

Arthropod A member of the invertebrate group with chitinous shells and jointed legs, including the crustaceans, insects, arachnids and centipedes.

Atrophy Wasting away of an organ that is no longer important, as a result of evolutionary development.

Bipedal Two-footed animal.

Carapace A thick, hard shell or shield that covers the body of some animals.

Carnosaur In old terminology, any big theropod, but in more modern terms a theropod belonging to the group that contains *Allosaurus* and its relatives.

Cartilaginous Referring to a skeleton composed entirely of cartilage, a tough, elastic tissue.

Cassowary A large flightless bird with a horny head crest and black plumage, from northern Australia.

Cenomanian A stage of the late Cretaceous period lasting from about 97 to 90 million years ago.

Ceratopsian Horned dinosaur.

Clade A group with common ancestry.

Cladogram A diagram illustrating the development of a clade.

Cololite A trace fossil consisting of the fossilized remains of the contents of an animal's digestive system.

Convergent evolution The evolutionary development of similar features on different animals that share the same environment.

Coprolite A trace fossil consisting of the fossilized remains of an animal's droppings.

Crest A tuft of fur, feathers or skin or a ridge of bone along the top of the head.

Cretaceous The last period of time in the Mesozoic era, which lasted 81 million years.

Cycad A tropical or subtropical plant with unbranched stalk and fern-like leaves crowded together at the top.

Dermal Relating to the skin.

Diapsid A member of a major group of the reptiles, classed by the presence of two holes in the skull behind the eye socket, and comprising the majority of modern reptiles including the lizards, snakes and crocodiles.

Digitigrade Walking so that only the toes touch the ground.

Diplodocid A herbivorous quadrupedal sauropod dinosaur from the late Jurassic or early Cretaceous periods, with a long neck and tail.

Dorsal Relating to the back or spine.

Fibula The outer thin bone from the knee to the ankle.

Gastralia A set of extra ribs covering the stomach area, as seen in some dinosaurs.

Gastrolith A stone in the stomach, deliberately swallowed to aid in digestion or buoyancy.

Gavial A type of fish-eating crocodile from South-east Asia.

Genus (genera pl.) A taxonomic group into which a family is divided and containing one or more species, all with a common characteristic.

Gizzard The thick-walled part of the stomach in which food is broken up by muscles and possibly gastroliths.

Gondwana (sometimes called Gondwanaland) The southern of two ancient continents, comprising modern-day Africa, Australia, South America, Antarctica and the Indian subcontinent. It was formed from the break-up of the supercontinent Pangaea 200 million years ago.

Groundmass A matrix of rock in which larger crystals are found.

Homeotherimic "Warm blooded", having the ability to keep the body at an almost constant temperature despite changes in the environment, as in mammals and birds, and probably some of the dinosaurs.

Humerus The bone from the shoulder to the elbow.

Ichnogenus A genus based only on fossil footprints.

Ichnology The study of fossil footprints.

Ichnospecies A species based only on fossil footprints.

Ichthyologist A scientist who studies fish.

Ischium A section of the hip bone which, in reptiles, sweeps backwards.

Isotope A form of the atom of a chemical element in which the atomic number is different from that of other atoms of the same element.

Jurassic The second period of the Mesozoic era and lasting for approximately 45 million years.

Keeled In a scale or an armour plate or a bone, having a ridge running along its length.

Keratinous Made up of keratin – a horny substance similar to fingernails.

Laurasia One of the two supercontinents formed by the break up of Pangaea 200 million years ago. It comprises modern North America, Greenland, Europe and Asia.

Lias The lowest series of rocks in the Jurassic system.

Maastrichtian The last age of the Cretaceous period, from 74 to 65 million years ago.

Megalosaur Large Jurassic or Cretaceous carnivorous bipedal dinosaur.

Mesozoic The era of geological time lasting from 245 to 65 million years ago and consisting of the Triassic, Jurassic and Cretaceous periods.

Nodule A small knot or lump – as a piece of armour bone embedded in the skin of an animal or as a mineral occurrence embedded in rock.

Nomen dubium Literally – "dubious name" – a name given to an animal that is not fully supported by scientific study.

Olecranon Bony projection behind the elbow joint.

Olfactory Relating to the sense of smell.

Olfactory bulb The point from which the nerves concerned with the sense of smell originate.

Ornithischian An order of dinosaurs that includes the ornithopods, stegosaurs, ankylosaurs and marginocephalians –

characterized by the hip bones, which are arranged like those of a bird.

Ornithomimid Bird-like, ostrich-mimic.

Ornithopod A herbivorous bipedal ornithischian dinosaur.

Ossicle A small bone.

Palaeogeography The study of what the geography was like in the past – the arrangement of the continents, the distribution of land and sea, and the climatic zones.

Palaeozoic The era of geological time that began 600 million years ago and lasted for 375 million years.

Paleontologist A scientist who studies fossils and the life of the past.

Pangaea The ancient supercontinent comprising all the present continents before they broke up 200 million years ago.

Petrifaction A process of forming fossils, particularly the process in which the organic matter of each cell of the creature is replaced by mineral.

Phalange A bone in the finger or toe.

Plantigrade Walking with the entire sole of the foot in contact with the ground.

Plate A thin sheet that forms an overlapping layer of protection.

Premaxilla The front bone of the upper jaw of dinosaurs.

Quadrupedal An animal that walks on all four limbs.

Refugium A geographical region that has remained unaltered by climate change.

Rostral Beak- or snout-like.

Saurischian An order of dinosaurs that includes the theropods, therizinosaurs, prosauropods and sauropods – characterized by the arrangement of hip bones, similar to those of a lizard.

Sauropod A herbivorous quadrupedal saurischian dinosaur, including *Apatosaurus*, *Diplodocus* and *Brachiosaurus*. Smallheads and long necks and tails characterize the group.

Scute A horny plate that makes up part of an armour.

Seismic Relating to earthquakes or earth tremors.

Silica The oxide of the element silicon, which is a major constituent of the minerals of the Earth's crust.

Species A taxonomic group into which a genus is divided.

Stegosaurid A quadrupedal herbivorous

ornithischian dinosaur, with bony plates and armour.

Stomach stone A gastrolith.

Swallow hole A depression in limestone terrain, usually into which a river or a stream disappears underground.

Synapsid A member of a major group of the reptiles, classed by the presence of a single combined hole in the skull behind the eye socket, and comprising the mammal-like reptiles from which the mammals evolved.

Symphysis A growing together of parts joined by an intermediary layer, particularly the join at the front of the lower jaw.

Taphonomy The study of what happens to a dead organism before it becomes buried and fossilized.

Taxonomy A system of classification of organisms.

Thecodont A reptile of Triassic times with teeth set in sockets. They gave rise to dinosaurs, crocodiles, pterodactyls and birds.

Theropod A bipedal carnivorous saurischian dinosaur.

Titanosaur A herbivorous quadrupedal sauropod dinosaur from the Cretaceous period.

Triassic The first period of the Mesozoic era, which lasted 37 million years.

Turbinal A folded bone inside the nose of some animals, supporting a membrane used to adjust the temperature or humidity of breathed air.

Ulna The inner and longer bone of the forearm.

Viviparous Giving birth to live offspring.

Wastebasket genus A genus to which many dubious fossils are attributed.

INDEX

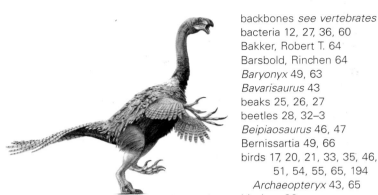

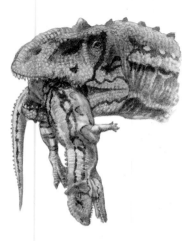

PICTURE ACKNOWLEDGEMENTS

The Publisher would like to thank the following picture agencies for granting permission to use their photographs in this book:
Key: l = left, r = right, t = top, c = centre, b = bottom

Alamy 28t, 32, 43, 53, 55
Ardea 10, 22, 28bl, 28br, 30t, 30b, 37tl, 37tr, 58, 62t, 62b, 63b
Corbis 45, 59br, 37br

The Natural History Museum 11, 33, 37bl, 63tr
David Varrichio 34

All illustration credits as follows:
Andrey Atuchin 24–5 main, 24bl, 25t, 27b, 61t, 72, 85
Peter Barrett 2, 8–9, 10, 11, 12–17, 21tr, 21bl, 23b, 25c, 26br, 27bc, 30, 31, 32, 33, 34, 35, 36, 38, 39b, 40–1, 42–3, 44, 45, 46–7, 48–9, 50–1, 52–3, 54–5, 58–9, 60b,

61bl, 61br, 64, 66–7, 68, 70, 76, 77, 80, 82, 84, 89, 91, 92, 93
Stuart Jackson-Carter 6b, 24bl, 24bc, 24br, 25bl, 25br, 25bc, 26bl, 26t, 56–7, 81
Julius T. Csotonyi www.csotonyi.com julius@ualberta.net, 1, 3, 6tr, 7t, 7b, 20–1 main, 21br, 21tl, 22–3 main, 23t, 27t, 27tl, 27br, 29, 39t, 71, 73, 74, 75, 79, 83, 86, 88, 90
Anthony Duke all maps and timelines.
Alain Beneteau 60t, 69, 78